Study Guide

to accompany

Fundamentals of Social Statistics

Third Edition

Kirk W. Elifson
Georgia State University

Richard P. Runyon

Audrey Haber

Prepared by
Philip Luck
Augusta State University

Kirk W. Elifson
Georgia State University

Boston   Burr Ridge, IL   Dubuque, IA   Madison, WI   New York   San Francisco   St. Louis
Bangkok   Bogotá   Caracas   Lisbon   London   Madrid
Mexico City   Milan   New Delhi   Seoul   Singapore   Sydney   Taipei   Toronto

McGraw-Hill

A Division of The **McGraw·Hill** *Companies*

Study Guide to accompany
FUNDAMENTALS OF SOCIAL STATISTICS

1 2 3 4 5 6 7 8 9 0 BKM/BKM 9 0 9 8 7

ISBN 0-07-290410-0

http://www.mhhe.com

TABLE OF CONTENTS

PREFACE

Each chapter of the *Study Guide to Accompany Fundamentals of Social Statistics* covers a corresponding chapter in your text. Use of this study guide will increase your understanding of relevant material covered in the text and your ability to master the statistical procedures within.

Each chapter of the study guide contains specific units. First, is a list of learning objectives providing a concise listing of the basic statistical concepts and principles presented in each chapter. These objectives are organized to follow the order of presentation of each chapter. Second, a programmed review gives sentence completion exercises for you to learn the use of the text. These exercises are organized within the learning objectives of the preceding section, and answers are presented to the right of each exercise. You are encouraged to conceal the answers while working through the exercises. Third, multiple-choice questions test your recall of the most important terms and concepts presented in each text chapter. As with the programmed review, answers appear at the right of each question. Finally, various thought problems review particular chapters. These thought problems underscore the concepts behind statistical procedures.

This study guide has been designed to help you learn and practice statistics, but is not intended as a substitute for the text. This supplement, used in conjunction with the text, should enhance your comprehension of the statistics course.

A word of thanks to Mary Lynne Glover, Robert Johnston, Allen Scarboro, Claire Sterk, and Mike Sweat for their assistance and support. Special thanks to Kirk Elifson, my friend and colleague, for the opportunity to participate in this project.

Philip A. Luck

Chapter 1

THE DEFINITION OF STATISTICAL ANALYSIS

Learning Objectives

After mastering the content of this chapter, you should be able to:

1. *Explain the uses of statistical knowledge in everyday life.*

2. *Define the terms most commonly used in statistics.*

3. *Describe the terms most commonly used in statistics.*

4. *Describe the basic procedures of inferential statistics.*

Programmed Review

Objective 1. *Explain the uses of statistical knowledge in everyday life.*

1. For many decisions in everyday life, we are required to assess the _____ of different outcomes.   **probabilities**

2. Statistics is the study of the formal procedures used for analyzing _____.   **data**

3. The statistical analysis of data helps us to make _____ and _____.   **decisions, inferences**

4. Statistics may be regarded as making summary statements about arithmetic properties of any _____ of facts.   **collection**

5. Statistics may also be regarded as a _____ for dealing with data.   **method**

6. Statements that present numerical information in the form of a convenient summary are called _____ statistics.   **descriptive**

7. Statements that generalize from samples to populations are called _____ statistics.   **inferential**

Objective 2. *Define the terms most commonly used in statistics.*

1. Any characteristic of a person, group, or environment that may assume different values is a _____.   **variable**

2. Any characteristic of a person, group, or environment that never changes is a _____.   **constant**

3. The numbers and measures that are collected as a result of scientific observation are called _____.   **data**

4. The term *data* is the plural for _____.   **datum**

5. A complete set of individuals, objects, or measurements having a common observable characteristic is a _____.   **population**

6. The data _____ based on a small population.   **are**

7. The data _____ that men are more violent than women.   **show**

8. We infer a parameter from a _____.   **statistic**

9.   Any measurable characteristic of a population is a _____.   **parameter**

10. A subset or part of a population is called a _____.   **sample**

11. A sample in which all elements have an equal chance of being selected is a _____ sample.   **random**

12. A number that describes a characteristic of a sample called a _____.   **statistic**

13. A statistic is frequently calculated from a sample in order to estimate a _____.   **population parameter**

14. Since parameters are rarely known it is necessary to estimate them from _____.   **sample statistics**

Objective 3.   *Describe the terms most commonly used in statistics.*

1.   The presentation of a variable that indicates the number of times each value occurs is called a _____.   **frequency distribution**

2.   Tables, graphs, and figures permit data to be displayed _____.   **visually**

3.   The descriptive statistics that describe the 'typical' score in a sample are measures of _____.   **central tendency**

4.   Descriptive statistics that measure the spread of scores around a central point are measures of _____.   **dispersion**

5.   Descriptive statistics that measure relationships between two different variables are called _____.   **correlations**

6.   A statistical procedure that permits prediction of one variable from another is called _____.   **regression analysis**

Objective 4.   *Describe the basic procedures of inferential statistics.*

1.   Inferential statistics are used to test _____.   **hypotheses**

2.   Inferential statistics are procedures for generalizing from samples to _____.   **populations**

3.   In the videotape vs. lecture study described in the text, the two treatment conditions were the _____ and _____ groups.   **experimental, control**

4.	When there is an average difference in the scores of experimental and control groups, inferential statistics attempt to eliminate explanations based on the factor of _____.	**chance**

5.	Inferential statistics are also known as _____ statistics.	**inductive**

6.	Inferential statistics are useful for arriving at conclusions that extend beyond _____ statistics.	**sample**

Multiple Choice Questions

1.	The numbers or measurements that are collected as the result of observation are called:	**b**

	a.	elements	c.	variables
	b.	data	d.	parameters

2.	The procedures used to organize and present data in convenient summaries are called:	**a**

	a.	descriptive statistics	c.	population parameters
	b.	inferential statistics	d.	dependent variables

3.	A single member of a population is:	**d**

	a.	a sample	c.	a variable
	b.	a statistic	d.	an element

4.	The value of a _____ never changes:	**a**

	a.	constant	c.	sample
	b.	variable	d.	population

5.	Procedures used to generalize from sample data to population parameters are called:	**c**

	a.	random samples	c.	inferential statistics
	b.	descriptive statistics	d.	independent variables

6.	Which of the following is not a goal of research:	**c**

	a.	information gathering	c.	labeling studies
	b.	describing relationships	d.	establishing causality

7. Establishing causality requires all but which of the following criteria:　　　**c**

    a. covariation
    b. time order
    c. independence
    d. eliminating alternative explanations

8. A complete set of individuals, objects, or measurements having some common observable characteristic is:　　　**d**

    a. a sample   c. data
    b. a constant   d. a population

9. Any characteristic of a person, group, or environment that can assume measurable differences is a:　　　**a**

    a. variable   c. statistic
    b. datum   d. parameter

10. A number that describes a mathematical characteristic of a sample is a:　　　**b**

    a. parameter   c. datum
    b. statistic   d. variable

11. The plan for collecting data is called the:　　　**c**
    a. descriptive function   c. research design
    b. inferential design   d. statistical analysis

12. A sample in which all elements have an equal chance of being selected is called:　　　**b**
    a. parametric   c. stratified
    b. simple random   d. matched

13. The two basic types of statistics are:　　　**c**

    a. prescriptive and descriptive
    b. inductive and deductive
    c. descriptive and inferential
    d. prescriptive and normative

14. In everyday life, people behave statistically when they estimate the _____ of different events.　　　**c**

    a. opportunity   c. likelihood
    b. variability   d. compatibility

15. Statistics that describe the distribution of scores about a   **b**
     central point are:

     a.   measures of central tendency
     b.   measures of dispersion
     c.   correlations
     d.   percentiles

16. Statistics that describe the 'typical' member of a sample   **a**
     or population are:

     a.   measures of central tendency
     b.   measures of dispersion
     c.   correlations
     d.   percentiles

17. Statistics that describe the relationship between two   **c**
     different variables are:

     a.   measures of central tendency
     b.   measures of dispersion
     c.   correlations
     d.   percentiles

18. Statistics that convert raw scores into rankings are called: **d**

     a.   measures of central tendency
     b.   measures of dispersion
     c.   correlations
     d.   percentiles

19. In order to estimate the ratio of males to females in a   **a**
     college, a sociology professor determines the proportion
     of males and females in his/her class. The resulting proportion is:

     a.   a statistic   c.   a percentile
     b.   a population   d.   a parameter

20. The total number of adults of voting age in the   **b**
     United States at any given time is:

     a.   a given   c.   a percentile
     b.   a population   d.   a parameter

21. When a television rating service reports, "Twenty-five million people, give or take two million, viewed a particular program," the statement represents:

    d

    a.   a wild guess   c.   a descriptive statistic
    b.   a sample statistic   d.   a statistical inference

22. In a complete census of a suburban community, it is reported that 53% of the families have two or more children. The 53% represents:

    a

    a.   a population parameter   c.   a sample parameter
    b.   a population statistic   d.   a statistical inference

23. Measurement of three individuals reveals their weight to be 120 lbs., 185 lbs., and 147 lbs. These numbers represent:

    a

    a.   values of a variable   c.   samples
    b.   statistics   d.   parameters

24. Unrest and violence on one Southern campus has decreased by 62% from 10 years ago. Four out of ten Americans brush their teeth twice daily. Hot Biscuits placed third in four of the twelve races last season.

After reading the above statements, select the correct answer below.

    c

    a.   These statements are derived from inductive statistics.
    b.   All of the given statements are sample parameters rather than population statistics.
    c.   Statistics, from one of its definitions, constitutes a collection of such statements.
    d.   These types of statements are usually found to be examples of lying with statistics.

25. Which of the following is not a variable:

    c

    a. $1-r^2$
    b.   John's blood pressure
    c.   the number of inches in a mile
    d. $5a + 2b - 3c$

26. The proportion of all male to female adults of legal driving age in the United States at a given time is a:

    b

    a.   statistic   c.   constant
    b.   parameter   d.   population

27. A scientist investigating the effects of environmental temperature   **c**
on the rate of chirping in crickets must draw the sample from the
population of:

     a.   all chirping insects
     b.   rate of chirping
     c.   all crickets
     d.   different sounds that crickets make

28. Which of the following is the correct use of the term "statistics?"   **d**

     a.   Claire bench-pressed 325 pounds.
     b.   Speaking of sales statistics, we sold $25,000 of merchandise
           last week.
     c.   At USA University, Melissa is just another statistic.
     d.   The average amount of student aid at USA University
           is $2,500.

29. A characteristic or phenomenon that may take on different values is   **d**
referred to as a:

     a.   constant   c.   data
     b.   parameter   d.   variable

30. A number resulting from the manipulation of data according to   **a**
specified procedures is called a:

     a.   statistic   c.   constant
     b.   parameter   d.   population

Chapter 2

BASIC MATHEMATICAL CONCEPTS

Learning Objectives

After mastering the content of this chapter, you should be able to:

1. *Describe the skills that are necessary for the mastery of statistics.*

2. *Explain the grammar of mathematical notation.*

3. *Describe the three different types of numbers and the four levels of measurement used in the development of scaling.*

4. *Explain the differences between discrete and continuous scales.*

5. *Explain the principals of rounding for the computation and presentation of statistical data.*

6. *Describe the use of ratios in the computation and presentation of statistical data.*

7. *Describe the uses of proportions, percentages, and rates in the computation and presentation of statistical data.*

Programmed Review

Objective 1. *Describe the skills that are necessary for the mastery of statistics.*

1. The degree of mathematical sophistication necessary for a firm grasp of the fundamentals of statistics is often _____.   **exaggerated**

2. Success in statistics requires little more than the mastery of several _____ and _____ procedures.   **algebraic, arithmetic**

Objective 2. *Explain the grammar of mathematical notation.*

1. X and Y are examples of mathematical _____.   **nouns**

2. The mathematical symbols X and Y are frequently used to identify _____.   **variables**

3. The symbol N represents the _____.   **number**

4. The mathematical symbol X_1 represents the use of a _____.   **subscript**

5. Notations that direct arithmetic operations are referred to as mathematical _____.   **verbs**

6. Mathematical verbs are commonly referred to as _____.   **operators**

7. The mathematical operator Σ is a symbol for _____.   **summation**

8. Notations that modify mathematical verbs are called mathematical _____.   **adverbs**

Objective 3. *Describe the three different types of numbers and the four levels of measurement used in the development of scaling.*

1. The numbers that are used to name objects or events are called _____ numbers.   **nominal**

2. The numbers that represent position in a series are called _____ numbers.   **ordinal**

3. In most of the statistical tests reported in this book, scaling is assumed at the _____ level.   **interval**

4. The assignment of numbers to objects or events according to sets of predetermined rules is called _____.

measurement

5. The objects or events that social scientists observe and measure are called _____.

variables

6. The particular observation of an object or event is called the _____ of the variable.

value

7. The rules for placing individuals or objects into unordered categories which are homogenous, mutually exclusive and exhaustive are _____ scales.

nominal

8. Data derived from nominal scales are most often called _____data or _____ data.

frequency, categorical

9. If the classes of measurement represent a rank-offered series of relationships, the resulting measurement is an _____ scale.

ordinal

10. The highest level of measurement in science is represented by _____ and _____ scales.

interval, ratio

11. The only difference between an interval scale and a ratio scale is that the interval scales have an arbitrary _____.

zero point

Objective 4. *Explain the difference between discrete and continuous scales.*

1. Scales with the basic characteristic of equality of counting units are called _____ scales.

discrete

2. Most of the discrete scales used by social scientists are expressed in terms of _____.

whole numbers

3. A scale in which a variable may assume an infinite number of intermediate values is called a _____ scale.

continuous

4. When continuous variables are expressed as whole numbers, they may appear to be _____.

discrete

5. The numerical values of continuously distributed variables are always _____.

approximate

6. The value of a continuous variable plus or minus one-half of the unit of measurement is the _____ of the variable.

true limit

Objective 5. *Explain the principals of rounding for the computation and presentation of statistical data.*

1. With respect to the rounding of decimal data, the policy proposed in the text is to round to two or more places than are in the _____ data.

   original

2. According to this rule, original data that are in whole-numbered units should be rounded to the _____ decimal.

   second

3. When rounding, the last digit should be increased to the next higher number if the remainder beyond that digit is greater than _____.

   five

4. When rounding, the last digit should remain unchanged if the remainder beyond that digit is less than _____.

   five

5. If the remainder beyond the last digit is exactly 5, the digit at the decimal place should be rounded to the nearest _____.

   even number

Objective 6. *Describe the use of ratios in the computation and presentation of statistical data.*

1. The division of one quantity by another results in a _____.

   ratio

2. The number of individuals per 100 younger than 15 or older than 64 relative to those between the ages of 15 and 64 is the _____.

   dependency ratio

3. According to the text, the dependency ratio for Vietnam is _____.

   81.5

4. According to the text, the dependency ratio for the United States is _____.

   53.8

5. According to the text, the ratio of whites to non-whites in the United States is about _____.

   4.8 : 1

Objective 7. *Describe the use of proportions, percentages, and rates in the computation and presentation of statistical data.*

1. The division of the quantity in one category by the total of all of the categories is a _____.

   proportion

2. Proportions may range in value from _____ to_____.

   0, 1

3.   When a proportion is multiplied by 100, it is converted into a   **percentage**
_____.

4.   The difference between the quantity at time 2 and the quantity   **percentage**
at time 1 divided by the quantity at time 1 is the_____.   **change**

5.   Percentage change is always computed   **base**
from an arbitrary _____.

6.   The number of occurrences in a group category divided by the   **rate**
total number of elements in a group is the _____.

Multiple Choice Questions

1.   The numbers that are used to name objects or events are   **c**
called _____ numbers.

     a.   cardinal   c.   nominal
     b.   ordinal   d.   continuous

2.   The numbers that are used to represent the position in a   **b**
series are called _____ numbers.

     a.   cardinal   c.   nominal
     b.   ordinal   d.   continuous

3.   Scales in which the variable can assume an infinite number   **c**
of intermediate values are called:

     a.   discrete scales   c.   continuous scales
     b.   ordinal scales   d.   nominal scales

4.   Scales in which the variables have an equality of   **a**
counting units are called _____ scales.

     a.   discrete   c.   continuous
     b.   ordinal   d.   nominal

5.   Scales in which the categories are homogenous, mutually   **d**
exclusive, exhaustive and unordered are called _____
scales.

     a.   ratio   c.   ordinal
     b.   interval   d.   nominal

6. Scales with arbitrary zero points on which exact distances are known are called _____ scales.   **b**

    a. ratio   c. ordinal
    b. interval   d. nominal

7. Scales with true zero points on which exact distance can be known are called _____ scales.   **a**

    a. ratio   c. ordinal
    b. interval   d. nominal

8. Scales in which the observations can be ranked are called _____ scales.   **c**

    a. ratio   c. ordinal
    b. interval   d. nominal

9. A proportion that has been multiplied by 100 is a: **b**

    a. rate   c. variable
    b. percentage   d. ratio

10. A value that is calculated by dividing the quantity in one category by the total of all the categories is the: **b**

    a. percentage   c. rate
    b. proportion   d. percentage change

11. A ratio of the occurrences in a group category to the total number of elements in the group is the: **c**

    a. percentage   c. rate
    b. proportion   d. percentage change

12. The value of a continuous variable plus or minus one-half the unit of measurement is the: **b**

    a. confidence interval   c. percentage change
    b. true limit   d. discrete scale

13. The assignment of numbers to objects or events according to sets of predetermined rules is: **b**

    a. observation   c. statistical analysis
    b. measurement   d. manipulation of variables

14

14. Any characteristic of an object or event that differs in a measurable way is a: **b**

    a. nominal scale   c. interval scale
    b. variable   d. proportion

15. The symbol Σ identifies the mathematical operation of: **a**

    a. summation   c. squaring
    b. subtraction   d. multiplication

16. Which of the following is *not* one of the three different uses of numbers identified in the text? **d**

    a. representing quantity
    b. representing serial position
    c. naming
    d. symbolizing abstract processes

17. Which of the following is the function of nominal numbers? **c**

    a. representing quantity
    b. representing serial position
    c. naming
    d. symbolizing abstract processes

18. Which of the following is the function of ordinal numbers? **b**

    a. representing quantity
    b. representing rank order
    c. naming
    d. symbolizing abstract processes

19. Any particular observation of a variable is called a: **b**

    a. ratio   c. symbol
    b. value   d. sign

20. Which of the following is not one of the four scales of measurement described in the text? **c**

    a. nominal   c. identity scales
    b. ordinal   d. ratio

21.   According to the text, the categories of nominal scales must: **b**

        a.   be heterogeneous
        b.   be mutually exclusive
        c   be mutually inclusive
        d.   assume ordered relationships between categories

22.   Sex, religious affiliation, and race are examples of   **a**
        _____ level variables.

        a.   nominal   c.   interval
        b.   ordinal   d.   ratio

23.   Frequency data and categorical data are most likely to   **a**
        be used with _____ scales.

        a.   nominal   c.   interval
        b.   ordinal   d.   ratio

24.   The categories used in ordinal scales must: **c**

        a.   be heterogeneous
        b.   be mutually exclusive
        c.   stand in some relationship to each other
        d.   have two zero points

25.   The classification of individuals on a measure of physical   **b**
        health would most likely be an example of:

        a.   a nominal scale   c.   an interval scale
        b.   an ordinal scale   d.   a ratio scale

26.   In attitude scaling, the Likert-type response categories   **b**
        of strongly disagree, disagree, agree, and strongly agree
        represent _____.

        a.   a nominal scale   c.   an interval scale
        b.   an ordinal scale   d.   a ratio scale

27.   A ratio scale differs from an interval scale in that the former: **b**

        a.   uses an arbitrary zero point
        b.   uses a true zero point
        c.   permits addition of quantities
        d.   permits subtraction of quantities

16

28. A person's height measured from the floor would be an example of _____ scale.   **d**

   a. a nominal   c. an interval
   b. an ordinal   d. a ratio

29. A person's height as measured from a table top would be an example of _____ scale.   **c**

   a. a nominal scale   c. an interval scale
   b. an ordinal scale   d. a ratio scale

30. Most of the statistical tests described in this book assume scaling at the _____ level.   **c**

   a. nominal   c. interval
   b. ordinal   d. ratio

31. According to the text, it is permissible to transform: **a**

   a. interval scales into ordinal scales
   b. nominal scales into ratio scales
   c. ordinal scales into ratio scales
   d. interval scales into ratio scales

32. The number of children per American family in an example of _____ scale.   **c**

   a. a nominal   c. a discrete
   b. an ordinal   d. a continuous

33. The number of members of a college fraternity is an example of _____ variable.   **c**

   a. a nominal   c. a discrete
   b. an ordinal   d. a continuous

34. According to the text, the most important characteristic of a discrete scale is: **b**

   a. use of whole numbers
   b. equality of counting units
   c. infinite number of possible values
   d. an arbitrary zero point

35. According to the text, the most important characteristic   **c**
    of a continuous scale is:

    a.   use of whole numbers
    b.   equality of counting units
    c.   infinite number of possible values
    d.   an arbitrary zero point

36. According to the text, the measurement of continuous variables: **a**

    a.   is always approximate
    b.   is always exact
    c.   requires advanced mathematical training
    d.   is always intermediate

37. Height and weight are examples of _____ variables.   **d**

    a.   nominal   c.   discrete
    b.   ordinal   d.   continuous

38. A number plus or minus one-half of the measurement   **d**
    unit is the _____ of a continuous variable.

    a.   range   c.   confidence interval
    b.   domain   d.   true limit

39. With respect to rounding, the policy proposed in the text is to   **a**
    round to _____ more places than appear in the original data.

    a.   two   c.   four
    b.   three   d.   five

40. If the original data appear in units of one-hundredths, you   **c**
    should round your answer to the _____ decimal.

    a.   second   c.   fourth
    b.   third   d.   fifth

41. If the remainder beyond the last digit is greater than 5, you should: **a**

    a.   increase the last digit to the next higher number
    b.   leave the last digit unchanged
    c.   decrease the last digit to the next lower number
    d.   drop the last digit entirely

42. If the remainder beyond the last digit is less than 5, you should: **b**

   a.   increase the last digit to the next higher number
   b.   leave the last digit unchanged
   c.   decrease the last digit to the next lower number
   d.   drop the last digit entirely

43. If the remainder beyond the last digit is exactly 5, you should round the last digit to the: **b**

   a.   nearest odd number   c.   farthest odd number
   b.   nearest even number   d.   farthest even number

44. If a city has 80 males per 100 females, the sex ratio is: **c**

   a.   180   c.   80
   b.   20   d.   1.25

45. If a small town has 50 persons younger than 15 or older than 64 and 100 persons between 15 and 64, its dependency ratio is: **c**

   a.   150   c.   50
   b.   100   d.   2

46. Proportions can range in value from: **c**

   a.   -100 to 100   c.   0 to +1
   b.   there is no range   d.   -1 to +1

47. When a proportion is multiplied by 100, it is converted into a: **a**

   a.   percentage   c.   ratio
   b.   percentile   d.   correlation

48. A percentage can assume values from: **c**

   a.   -100 to 100   c.   0 to 100
   b.   -1 to +1   d.   -50 to 50

49. In the computation of percentage change, the base number is always the: **a**

   a.   quantity at time 1
   b.   quantity at time 2
   c.   quantity at time 1 minus quantity at time 2
   d.   quantity at time 1 plus quantity at time 2

50. Birth rates are customarily reported as the number of births per _____ people.   **c**

   a. 10   c. 1000
   b. 100   d. 100,000

51. The number 15.00500 rounded to the second decimal place is: **a**

   a. 15.00   c. 15.005
   b. 15.05   d. 16

52. The number 43.54499 rounded to the second decimal place is: **a**

   a. 43.54   c. 43.60
   b. 43.55   d. none of the above

53. $\dfrac{a+b}{c}$ equals: **a**

   a. $\dfrac{a}{c}+\dfrac{b}{c}$ c. $c(a+b)$

   b. $\dfrac{ac+b}{a+c}$ d. none of the above

54. $\dfrac{a}{b+c}$ equals: **d**

   a. $\dfrac{a}{b}+\dfrac{b}{c}$ c. $c(a+b)$

   b. $\dfrac{ac+b}{a+c}$ d. none of the above

55. $\dfrac{X^5}{X^2}$ equals: **c**

   a. $X^5 - X^2$ c. X^3
   b. $5X - 2X$ d. X^7

56. Y^0 equals: **a**

   a. 1   c. $Y + 0$
   b. $Y/0$ d. must know value of Y

57. The data employed with interval or ratio scales are frequently referred to as: **b**

   a. head counts   c. ranks
   b. scores   d. ordinal position

Thought Problems

Identity the levels of scaling that are most likely to be obtained in the measurement of the following variables.

1. Number of men and women enrolled at particular college.

2. Classification of persons as either Protestants, Catholics, or Jews.

3. The measurement of the height of persons in inches.

4. The measurement of the weight of persons in pounds.

5. The measurement of a person's physical health.

6. The measurement of a person's family income.

7. The measurement of temperature on the Fahrenheit scale.

8. The measurement of a person's intelligence in IQ points.

9. Classification of students as seniors, juniors, sophomores, and freshpersons.

10. Classification of attitudes into the categories of 'strongly' agree', 'agree', 'disagree', 'strongly disagree'.

State whether each of the following variables is more likely to be measured on discrete or continuous scales.

11. Annual family income.

12. Cups of coffee sold in a college cafeteria.

13. The weight of persons measured in pounds.

14. The number of children per family.

15. Number of books in a college library.

16. A person's times for running a 100-meter dash.

17. A person's skin color.

18. A person's scores on an IQ test.

19. Temperatures in different regions of the country.

Answers to Thought Problems

1.	ratio	8.	interval	15.	discrete
2.	nominal	9.	ordinal	16.	continuous
3.	ratio	10.	ordinal	17.	continuous
4.	ratio	11.	discrete	18.	discrete
5.	ordinal	12.	discrete	19.	continuous
6.	ratio	13.	discrete		
7.	interval	14.	discrete		

Chapter 3

FREQUENCY DISTRIBUTIONS AND GRAPHING TECHNIQUES

Learning Objectives

After mastering the content of this chapter, you should be able to:

1. *Describe how large amounts of data are grouped into frequency distributions.*

2. *Explain how cumulative frequency and cumulative percentage distributions are constructed from grouped frequency distributions.*

3. *Explain the misuses of graphing techniques.*

4. *Describe the graphing techniques used for nominally scaled variables, ordinally scaled variables, and interval and ratio scaled variables.*

5. *Describe the different forms of frequency curves.*

6. *Describe several additional forms for the graphic representation of data.*

Programmed Review

Objective 1. *Describe how large amounts of data are grouped into frequency distributions.*

1. When the values of a variable are ordered according to their magnitudes, the number of times that each score occurs is shown by a _____.

    frequency distribution

2. In a grouped frequency distribution, the values of the variables are grouped into separate _____.

    class intervals

3. When data are grouped into class intervals, the scale must be _____.

    collapsed

4. In a grouped frequency distribution, the classes to which the scores are assigned must be _____ and _____.

    mutually exclusive, exhaustive

5. The requirement of mutual exclusiveness means that each score is assigned to one and only one _____.

    class interval

6. The requirement of exhaustiveness means that a class interval must be available for the assignment of each _____.

    score

7. The grouping of scores into grouped frequency distribution means the loss of _____.

    information

8. When individual scores are grouped into class intervals they lose their _____.

    identity

9. In a grouped frequency distribution, the symbol i designates the _____ of the class interval.

    width

10. The lowest class interval in a frequency distribution ranges from the lowest score in the original data to the lowest score plus _____.

    $i - 1$

Objective 2. *Explain how cumulative frequency and cumulative percentage distributions are constructed from grouped frequency distributions.*

1. A cumulative frequency distribution shows the cumulative frequency below the upper real limit of the corresponding _____.

    class interval

2. A cumulative frequency distribution is valuable for illustrating the _____ of scores.

    percentile ranks

3. The frequency of park visitors falling within each class interval is indicated by the symbol_____.   *f*

4. The bottom entry in a cumulative frequency column is always equal to _____.   *N*

5. When each entry in the cumulative *f* column is divided by *N*, the result is a _____ distribution.   **cumulative proportion**

6. When each cumulative proportion is multiplied by 100, the result is a _____.   **cumulative percentage**

7. The bottom entry in the cumulative proportion column must be equal to _____.   **1**

8. The bottom entry in the cumulative % column must be equal to _____.   **100%**

Objective 3. *Explain the uses and misuses of graphing techniques.*

1. After the construction of a frequency distribution, the next step is to present the data in _____.   **pictorial form**

2. Pictorial presentations of data are called _____.   **graphs**

3. Graphs are best interpreted as _____ for thinking about data.   **visual aids**

4. The selection of units for the *X* and *Y*-axis of a graph is the result of _____.   **arbitrary choice**

Objective 4. *Describe the graphing techniques used for nominally scaled variables, ordinally scaled variables, and interval and ratio scaled variables.*

1. A graphic device used to represent data that are nominally or ordinally scaled is the _____.   **bar graph**

2. In a bar graph, the number of members of a class is represented by the _____ of the bar.   **height**

3. In a bar graph, the frequency of each category is represented by the _____ of each bar.   **area**

4. In a bar graph, the total area of all the bars is equal to _____.   *N*

5. For nominally scaled variables, the categories represented along the horizontal axis of a bar graph should be ordered _____.   **alphabetically**

6. For nominally scaled variables, the bars of a bar graph should be _____.   **separated**

7. The vertical bars are permitted to touch one another in graphic representations of variables scaled at the _____and _____levels of measurement.   **interval, ratio**

8. The graph described in the previous statement is called a _____.   **histogram**

9. In dealing with continuous variables, it is advisable to construct histograms with equal _____.   **intervals**

10. The histogram is most frequently converted into a _____.   **frequency curve**

11. To convert a histogram into a frequency curve, it is necessary to draw straight lines between the _____ of the bars.   **midpoints**

12. In practice, the histogram is preferred to the frequency curve for variables that are distributed _____.   **discretely**

13. In practice, the frequency curve is preferred to the histogram for variables that are distributed _____.   **continuously**

14. The cumulative frequency curve is called an _____.   **ogive**

Objective 5. *Describe the different forms of frequency curves.*

1. A bell-shaped frequency curve is called a _____ curve.   **normal**

2. A frequency curve with extra scores in the center of the distribution is called a _____ distribution.   **leptokurtic**

3. A frequency curve with extra scores at the ends of the distribution is called a _____ distribution.   **platykurtic**

4. A frequency curve that resembles a normal curve is called a _____ distribution.   **mesokurtic**

5. The normal curve is referred to as a _____ distribution.   **symmetrical**

6. However, not all symmetrical distributions are _____.   **normal**

7. An important form of nonnormal symmetrical curves is the _____ distribution.   **rectangular**

8.   When a nonsymmetrical distribution "tails" off to the right it is   **skewed**
       said to be _____

9.   A nonsymmetrical distribution that "tails" off to the right is said   **positively**
       to be _____ skewed.

10.   A nonsymmetrical distribution that "tails" off to the left is said   **negatively**
       to be _____ skewed.

Objective 6. *Describe several additional forms for the graphic representation of data.*

1.   The adaptation of the bar graph that is frequently used to depict   **pictograph**
       data is the _____.

2.   The division of a circle into its component parts in order to represent   **pie chart**
       the distribution of a nominal level variable is a _____.

3.   In a pie chart, each 1% of the distribution is equal to _____.   **3.6 degrees**

4.   In the description of data, the projection of future events   **trend chart**
       requires the use of a_____.

Multiple Choice Questions

1.   A representation of the number of times that each score occurs   **c**
       when the values of a variable are ordered is a:

       a.   leptokurtic distribution
       b.   negatively skewed distribution
       c.   frequency distribution
       d.   normal distribution

2.   In a grouped frequency distribution, the scores are organized   **c**
       into _____.

       a.   random patterns   c.   class intervals
       b.   comparative ratios   d.   ordinal scales

3.   The class intervals that are used for the graphing of scores   **b**
       must be:

       a.   mutually inclusive and reciprocal
       b.   mutually exclusive and exhaustive
       c.   mutually exclusive and balanced
       d.   exhaustive and balanced

4. Which of the following is not one of the reasons for grouping scores into intervals?   **c**

    a. absence of automatic calculators
    b. elimination of scores with excessively low frequency counts
    c. elimination of scores with excessively high frequency counts
    d. needs for meaningful summary of the data

5. The first step in the construction of a grouped frequency distribution is to obtain the: **b**

    a. sum of the highest and lowest scores
    b. difference between the highest and lowest scores
    c. product of the highest and lowest scores
    d. ratio of the highest and lowest scores

6. In the construction of a grouped frequency distribution, the symbol i designates the: **c**

    a. total number of scores
    b. total number of class intervals
    c. width of the class interval
    d. width of the entire distribution

7. The limits of the lowest class interval are the lowest score in the original data to the same score plus: **b**

    a. $i - 2$ c. i
    b. $i - 1$ d. $i + 1$

8. The true limits of a class interval of 30 to 34 with whole numbers as the unit of measurement is: **b**

    a. 30 to 34   c. 29 to 35
    b. 29.5 to 34.5   d. 29.5 to 34

9. A cumulative frequency distribution shows the cumulative frequency: **c**

    a. below the lower true limit of the corresponding class interval
    b. above the lower true limit of the corresponding class interval
    c. below the upper true limit of the corresponding class interval
    d. above the upper true limit of the corresponding class interval

10. The bottom entry in the cumulative frequency column of a cumulative frequency distribution is always equal to: **c**

    a. i c. N
    b. f d. $i - 1$

11. In a cumulative frequency distribution, the division of each entry in the cumulative *f* column by *N* yields the cumulative _____ distribution. **d**

   a. ratio
   b. percentage
   c. interval
   d. proportion

12. When each cumulative proportion is multiplied by 100, we obtain a cumulative _____ distribution. **c**

   a. ratio
   b. interval
   c. percentage
   d. normal

13. In a cumulative percentage distribution, the bottom entry in the cumulative proportion column must equal to: **c**

   a. 20%
   b. 50%
   c. 100%
   d. 200%

14. In the cumulative proportion distribution, the bottom entry in the cumulative proportion column must equal: **b**

   a. 0
   b. 1
   c. 50
   d. 100

15. The visual presentation of statistical data that uses a *Y*-axis and an *X*-axis is the: **d**

   a. chart
   b. picture
   c. pictograph
   d. graph

16. The *X*-axis of a graph is placed on the _____ axis. **c**

   a. normal distribution
   b. vertical
   c. horizontal
   d. coordinate

17. The *Y*-axis of a graph is placed on the _____ axis. **d**

   a. normal distribution
   b. coordinate
   c. horizontal
   d. vertical

18. The bar graph is a graphic device used to represent data that are scaled at the: **d**

   a. nominal and ratio levels
   b. ordinal and interval levels
   c. interval and ratio levels
   d. nominal and ordinal levels

19. In a bar graph, the number of cases in each class is represented by the _____ of the bar. **a**

    a. height   c. area
    b. width   d. perimeter

20. In a bar graph, N is equal to the _____ of all the bars. **c**

    a. height   c. area
    b. width   d. perimeter

21. In a bar graph of nominally scaled variables, the categories should be arranged: **c**

    a. according to the magnitude of the variable
    b. in alphabetical order
    c. according to the personal preferences of the statistician
    d. from the smallest to largest

22. In a bar graph of nominal data, the implication of continuity among the categories is avoided by: **b**

    a. using different colors for the bars
    b. separating the bars
    c. drawing bars of different height
    d. drawing bars of different width

23. In a bar graph of ordinal data, the categories should be placed in their naturally occurring order along the: **a**

    a. horizontal axis   c. 30 degree axis
    b. vertical axis   d. 60 degree axis

24. A bar graph of interval- and ratio-scaled variables is called a(n): **c**

    a. pictogram   c. histogram
    b. frequency curve   d. ogive

25. When the midpoints of the bars of the histogram are connected with straight lines, the result is a: **a**

    a. frequency curve   c. platykurtic distribution
    b. frequency polygon   d. leptokurtic distribution

26. A cumulative frequency curve that shows the number of cases below the true limit of an interval is:

    c

  a.   a normal curve   c.   an ogive
  b.   an ordinate   d.   a skewed distribution

27. A distribution of scores that takes the bell-shaped form of a normal curve is a _____distribution.

    d

  a.   rectangular   c.   platykurtic
  b.   leptokurtic   d.   mesokurtic

28. When scores are piled up in the center of a distribution, the result is a _____distribution.

    b

  a.   rectangular   c.   platykurtic
  b.   leptokurtic   d.   mesokurtic

29. When scores are piled up at the extremes of a distribution, the result is a _____distribution.

    c

  a.   normal   c.   platykurtic
  b.   leptokurtic   d.   mesokurtic

30. The normal curve is referred to as_____distribution.

    a

  a.   a symmetrical   c.   a bimodal
  b.   an asymmetrical   d.   a mesokurtic

31. A nonsymmetrical distribution is said to be:

    c

  a.   bimodal   c.   skewed
  b.   rectangular   d.   irregular

32. A nonsymmetrical distribution that "tails" off to the right side is said to be

    c

  a.   rectangular   c.   positively skewed
  b.   platykurtic   d.   negatively skewed

33. A nonsymmetrical distribution that "tails" off to the left side is said to be:

    d

  a.   rectangular   c.   positively skewed
  b.   platykurtic   d.   negatively skewed

34. A graphic presentation that is adapted directly from the bar graph is the: **b**

   a. ogive c. pie chart
   b. pictograph d. trend chart

35. The division of a circle into component parts in order to represent the distribution of a variable is a: **c**

   a. ogive c. pie chart
   b. pictograph d. trend chart

36. A projection of time-series data from the past or into the future requires a _____. **d**

   a. ogive c. pie chart
   b. pictograph d. trend chart

37. In a pie chart, 1% of the variable under study equals _____ degrees. **b**

   a. 1.8 c. 7.2
   b. 3.6 d. 14.4

38. The true limits of the score 6 are: **c**

   a. 6.0 - 7.0 c. 5.5 - 6.5
   b. 5.0 - 6.0 d. 5.9 - 6.1

39. If our lowest score were 19 and the highest score were 82 and we decided to group our scores into 8 intervals, what would the width of each interval be? **a**

   a. 8 c. 9
   b. 10 d. not enough information

40. The true limits of the interval 80 - 84 are: **d**

   a. 0 - 4 c. 79 - 85
   b. 80.5 - 83.5 d. 79.5 -84.5

41. The midpoint of the interval 20 - 23 is: **b**

   a. 21 c. 22
   b. 21.5 d. none of the above

42. The midpoint of an interval with a width of 7 is 12. The upper apparent limit is: **c**

    a.   14   c.   15
    b.   14.5   d.   15.5

43. If there are ten class intervals in a frequency distribution, and the apparent lowest interval is 2 - 4, the apparent highest class interval is: **d**

    a.   26 - 27   c.   27 - 30
    b.   26 - 28   d.   29 - 31

44. The midpoint of the interval 12 - 21 is: **d**

    a.   15   c.   16
    b.   15.5   d.   16.5

45. The midpoint of a class with a width of 5 is 20. The lower true limit is: **c**

    a.   16.5   c.   17.5
    b.   17   d.   18

46. In a cumulative frequency curve, each frequency in plotted over: **b**

    a.   the midpoint of the class   c.   the lower real limit of the class
    b.   the upper real limit of the class   d.   the frequency corresponding to the class

47. When we arrange a set of scores in order of magnitude and indicate the frequency associated with each score, we have constructed: **d**

    a.   a grouped frequency distribution
    b.   a frequency curve
    c.   a histogram
    d.   an ungrouped frequency distribution

48. The upper true limits of the class intervals 0-4, 5-9, and 10-14 are: **c**

    a.   4.1, 9.1, 14.1   c.   4.5, 9.5, 14.5
    b.   4, 9, 14   d.   4.5, 9, 14.1

49. The limits of a class interval are 15 - 32. The width of the class is: **d**

    a.   15   c.   17
    b.   16   d.   18

50. It is generally agreed that most data in the social sciences can be accommodated by how many classes?   **c**

   a.   5 - 10   c.   10 - 20
   b.   10 - 12   d.   15 - 30

51. A student prepares a frequency distribution with six categories. Which of the following problems is most likely to arise?   **b**

   a.   Extreme values will be given undue weight in computing central tendency
   b.   Final statistical values will contain excessive error because of grouping
   c.   Final statistical values will contain excessive error because of rounding
   d.   Scores that do not fall in the class will have to be eliminated

Chapter 4

PERCENTILES

Learning Objectives

After mastering the content of this chapter, you should be able to:

1.   *Explain the concept of percentile rank.*

2.   *Describe the uses and the computation of cumulative percentiles and percentile ranks.*

3.   *Describe the uses and computations of centiles, deciles, and quartiles.*

Programmed Review

Objective 1. *Explain the concept of percentile rank.*

1.	The percentage of scores lower than a specific score is the _____.	**percentile rank**
2.	The percentile rank provides a _____for the interpretation of any specific score.	**frame of reference**
3.	To say that an age of 65 has percentile rank of 88 indicates that _____ of the population is 65 or less.	**88%**

Objective 2. *Describe the uses and the computation of cumulative percentiles and percentile ranks.*

1.	Percentile ranks can be read directly as a _____.	**percentage distribution**
2.	A graphic form of the cumulative percentage distribution is an _____.	**ogive**
3.	The percentile rank of a score is defined symbolically as _____.	$\dfrac{\text{cum } f}{N} \times 100$
4.	In the generalized equation for the calculation of percentile rank, the cumulative frequency at the lower limit of the interval containing X is symbolized as _____.	$\text{cum } f_{ll}$
5.	In the generalized equation for the calculation of percentile rank, the given score is symbolized as _____.	X
6.	In the generalized equation for the calculation of percentile rank, the score at the lower true limit of the interval containing X is symbolized as _____.	X_{ll}
7.	In the generalized equation for the calculation of percentile rank, the width of the interval is symbolized as _____.	i
8.	In the generalized equation for the calculation of percentile rank, the number of cases within the interval containing X is symbolized as _____.	f_i
9.	In the generalized equation for determining scores from percentiles, the score at the lower real limit of the interval containing cum f is symbolized as _____.	X_{ll}

10. In the generalized equation for determining scores from percentiles, the cumulative frequency of the score is symbolized as _____. **cum _f_**

11. In the generalized equation for determining scores from percentiles, the cumulative frequency at the lower real limit of the interval containing cum _f_ is symbolized as _____. **cum f_{ll}**

12. In the generalized equation for determining scores from percentiles, the number of cases within the interval containing cum _f_ is symbolized as _____. **f_i**

13. A percentile rank must always be expressed in relation to some _____. **reference group**

14. When computing percentile ranks or scores from percentiles we assume that the cases or frequencies within a particular interval are evenly distributed throughout that _____. **interval**

Objective 3. *Describe the uses and computations of centiles, deciles, and quartiles.*

1. A percentile rank that divides a distribution into 100 equal parts is a _____. **centile**

2. A percentile rank that divides a distribution into 10 equal parts is a _____. **decile**

3. A percentile rank that divides a distribution into four equal parts is a _____. **quartile**

4. The seventh centile is specified as _____. **C_7**

5. The fifth decile is specified as _____. **D_5**

6. The second quartile is specified as _____. **Q_2**

7. On any scale of percentile ranks, there will be _____ centiles, _____ deciles, and _____ quartiles. **99, 9, 3**

Multiple Choice Questions

1. A percentage rank that divides a distribution into 100 equal parts is the: **b**

   a. decile   c. quartile
   b. centile   d. quintile

2.   A percentage rank that divides a distribution into 10   **a**
      equal parts is the:

      a.   decile   c.   quartile
      b.   centile   d.   quintile

3.   A percentage rank that divides a distribution into four   **c**
      equal parts is the:

      a.   decile   c.   quartile
      b.   centile   d.   quintile

4.   The percentile is the same as the: **a**

      a.   centile   c.   quartile
      b.   decile   d.   quintile

5.   The number that represents the percentage of cases in a   **b**
      distribution with scores below the score in question is the:

      a.   decile   c.   quartile
      b.   percentile rank   d.   centile

6.   Percentile ranks may be obtained directly from examination of: **b**

      a.   grouped frequency distributions
      b.   cumulative percentage distributions
      c.   leptokurtic distributions
      d.   platykurtic distributions

7.   The graphic form of a cumulative percentage distribution   **a**
      is called:

      a.   an ogive   c.   a histogram
      b.   a bar graph   d.   a pictograph

8.   In the generalized equation for the calculation of percentile ranks, **b**
      X is the:

      a.   width of the interval
      b.   given score
      c.   number of cases within the interval containing X is the
      d.   the score at the lower true limit of the interval containing X

9. In the generalized equation for the calculation of percentile ranks, the symbol i is the: **a**

    a. width of the interval
    b. given score
    c. number of cases within the interval containing X
    d. the score at the lower true limit of the interval containing X

10. In the generalized equation for the calculation of percentile ranks, the symbol X_{ll} is the: **d**

    a. width of the interval
    b. given score
    c. number of cases within the interval containing X
    d. the score at the lower true limit of the interval containing X

11. In the generalized equation for the calculation of percentile ranks, the symbol f_i is the: **c**

    a. width of the interval
    b. given score
    c. number of cases within the interval containing X
    d. the score at the lower true limit of the interval containing X

12. In the generalized equation for determining scores from percentiles, the symbol X_{ll} is the: **b**

    a. width of the interval
    b. score at the lower true limit of the interval containing cum f
    c. cumulative frequency of the score
    d. number of cases within the interval containing cum f

13. In the generalized equation for determining scores from percentiles, the symbol i is the: **a**

    a. width of the interval
    b. score at the lower true limit of the interval containing cum f
    c. cumulative frequency of the score
    d. number of cases within the interval containing cum f

14. In the generalized equation for determining scores from percentiles, the symbol cum f is the: **c**

    a. width of the interval
    b. score at the lower true limit of the interval containing cum f
    c. cumulative frequency of the score
    d. number of cases within the interval containing cum f

15. In the generalized equation for determining scores from percentiles, the symbol f_i is the:

 a. width of the interval
 b. score at the lower real limit of the interval containing cum f
 c. cumulative frequency of the score
 d. number of cases within the interval containing cum f

d

16. A percentile rank must always be expressed in relation to a specific:

 a. frequency distribution   c. pictograph
 b. reference group   d. trend chart

b

17. In any scale of percentile ranks, there are _____ deciles.

 a. 9   c. 11
 b. 10   d. 12

a

18. In any scale of percentile ranks, there are _____ quartiles.

 a. 2   c. 4
 b. 3   d. 5

b

19. In any scale of percentile ranks, there are _____ centiles.

 a. 99   c. 101
 b. 100   d. 102

a

20. The third quartile corresponds to the _____ centile.

 a. 25th   c. 75th
 b. 50th   d. 99th

c

21. If the percentile rank of a score of 20 is 65, we may say that:

 a. 20% of a comparison group scores at or below 65
 b. 20% of a comparison group scored above 65
 c. 65% of a comparison group scored above 20
 d. 65% of a comparison group scored at or below 20

d

22. Assume that there are 10 cases in the class interval 1 - 5. The score that corresponds to a cumulative frequency of 7 is:

 a. 4.5   c. 3.0
 b. 2.6   d. 4.0

d

23. In the above example, the cumulative frequency of a score of 2 is: **b**

   a.   1   c.   4
   b.   3   d.   5

24. When we convert scores to percentile ranks and vice versa, we are performing: **c**

   a.   a curvilinear transformation
   b.   a cumulative transformation
   c.   a linear transformation
   d.   a grouping conversion

25. An individual's score has a percentile rank of 90 on an achievement exam. This means that he or she: **b**

   a.   had twice as many times right as someone with a percentile rank of 45
   b.   performed as well as or better than 90% of the group taking the test
   c.   placed ninetieth in the group taking the test
   d.   impossible to answer without more information

26. A student obtained a score of 80 on a statistics test, placing the student at the 88th percentile. If 10 points were added to each score in the distribution, the new score for the student whose score became 90 would be at the: **c**

   a.   90th percentile   c.   88th percentile
   b.   98th percentile   d.   None of the above

27. The statistic that represents the percentage at and below a specific value is a: **d**

   a.   quartile   c.   median
   b.   quintile   d.   percentile

Use the following grouped frequency and cumulative distributions of scores to answer questions 28 through 33.

Class	f	Cum f
0 - 5	2	2
6 - 11	6	8
12 - 17	10	18
18 - 23	16	34
24 - 29	8	42
30 - 35	5	47
36 - 41	3	50

28.   The class width is: **d**

a.   4   c.   5.5
b.   5   d.   6

29.   For this sample, $N =$ **d**

a.   25   c.   40
b.   30   d.   50

30.   The score at the 40th percentile is in the class interval: **c**

a.   6 - 11   c.   18 - 23
b.   12 - 17   d.   24 - 29

31.   The score with a percentile rank of 50 is in the class: **c**

a.   30 - 35   c.   18 - 23
b.   24 - 29   d.   6 - 11

32.   The score of 13 has an approximate percentile rank of: **d**

a.   17.0   c.   15.3
b.   25.0   d.   21.0

33.   A score of 23.5 has a percentile rank of: **c**

a.   32.0   c.   68.0
b.   16.0   d.   65.4

Chapter 5

MEASURES OF CENTRAL TENDENCY

Learning Objectives

After mastering the content of this chapter, you should be able to:

1. *Discuss the uses of the word "average" and describe the basic characteristics of frequency distributions.*

2. *Define the mean and describe its algebraic properties.*

3. *Define the median and explain how it is computed for grouped and ungrouped scores.*

4. *Define the mode and describe the characteristics of unimodal, bimodal, and multimodal distributions.*

5. *Compare the statistical characteristics of the mean, median, and mode.*

6. *Describe the effects of skewness on the mean, median, and mode.*

Programmed Review

Objective 1. *Discuss the uses of the word "average" and describe the basic characteristics of frequency distributions.*

1. As a substitute for the word average, statisticians speak of measures of _____.

    central tendency

2. We may define central tendency as a location used in the description of a _____.

    frequency distribution

3. There are several different measures of central tendency because the _____ of a distribution may be defined in different ways.

    center

4. The three most frequently used measures of central tendency are the _____, _____ , and _____.

    mean, median, mode

5. Symmetry and skewness are measures of the _____ of a frequency distribution.

    form

6. Frequency data cluster around a _____.

    central value

7. Frequency data can be characterized by their degree of _____ around a central value.

    dispersion

Objective 2. *Define the mean and describe its algebraic properties.*

1. The sum of the scores divided by the number of scores is the arithmetic _____.

    mean

2. In order to compute the mean, scores must be obtained at the _____ level of measurement.

    interval

3. In the equation for the mean, N is the _____.

    number of scores

4. In the equation for the mean, ΣX is called the _____.

    sum of the scores

5. The equation for the arithmetic mean from an ungrouped frequency distribution is _____.

    $\bar{X} = \Sigma fX/N$

6. To compute the mean from a grouped frequency distribution, it is assumed that each score lies at the _____ of its interval.

    midpoint

7.   The computation of the mean from the midpoints of intervals assumes that the scores in each interval are _____. **evenly distributed**

8.   The distance of each score from the mean is its _____. **deviation**

9.   When a score is larger than the mean, the result is a _____ deviation. **positive**

10. When a score is smaller than the mean, the result is a _____ deviation. **negative**

11. The algebraic sum of the mean deviations of all scores is _____. **zero**

12. The value of the mean is sensitive to _____. **extreme scores**

13. The sum of all the squared deviations around the mean is _____. **minimal**

14. When positive and negative values are squared, the result

     is a _____. **positive value**

15. The grand mean of a set of two or more means requires the computation of the _____. **weighted mean**

Objective 3.   *Define the median and explain how it is computed for grouped and ungrouped scores.*

1.   The score above and below which one-half of the frequencies fall is the _____. **median**

2.   The median is the score at the _____. **50th percentile**

3.   If N is an odd number, the median is the _____ in the distribution. **middle value**

4.   If N is an even number, the median is the arithmetic mean of the two_____. **middle values**

5.   The lowest level of measurement that permits computation of the median is the _____ level. **ordinal**

6. When the middle score of a distribution is tied with several other scores, the easiest procedure is to convert all scores into an _____ distribution.

    ungrouped frequency

7. An important characteristic of the median is its _____ to extreme scores.

    insensitivity

8. The median is the most valuable description of central tendency when the _____ is unacceptable.

    mean

Objective 4. *Define the mode and describe the characteristics of unimodal, bimodal, and multimodal distributions.*

1. The mode is the score that occurs with _____.

    greatest frequency

2. For grouped data, the mode is the midpoint of the interval containing the highest _____.

    frequency count

3. In a histogram the mode is represented by the midpoint of the _____.

    tallest column

4. The lowest level of measurement for which the mode can be determined is the _____ level.

    nominal

5. For categorical data, the mode is located in the category with the _____ of cases.

    plurality

6. From a statistical perspective, the mode is also the most _____ value.

    probable

7. A distribution with two modes is called _____.

    bimodal

8. A distribution with more than two modes is called _____.

    multimodal

Objective 5. *Compare the statistical characteristics of the mean, median, and mode.*

1. In general, the preferred statistic for representing the central tendency is the _____.

    mean

2. The mean is the preferred measure of central tendency if the distribution of scores is not _____.

    skewed

3. The most stable and reliable measure of central tendency is the _____.

    mean

4.	The stability of a statistic is important in the effort to infer from a sample to a _____.	**population**
5.	The mean, median, and mode are identical in a _____ distribution.	**symmetrical**
6.	A distribution in which the mean is larger than the median is _____.	**positively skewed**
7.	A commonly studied variable that is positively skewed is annual _____.	**family income**
8.	The statistic that can be used with all levels of measurement is the _____.	**mode**
9.	Variables must be measured at the ordinal level or higher for the computation of the _____.	**median**

Objective 6. *Describe the effects skewness on the mean, median, and mode.*

1.	When the mean is larger than the median, the distribution is _____.	**positively skewed**
2.	When the mean is smaller than the median, the distribution is _____.	**negatively skewed**
3.	The tail of a positively skewed distribution runs to the _____.	**right**
4.	The tail of a negatively skewed distribution runs to the _____.	**left**
5.	The measure of central tendency that is seldom used in social science research is the _____.	**mode**

Multiple Choice

1.	In the study of statistics, the word "average" is replaced by the concept of:	**b**

    a.   dispersion   c.   frequency
    b.   central tendency   d.   skewness

2.	Which of the following is *not* a measure of central tendency?	**c**

    a.   the median   c.   the middle
    b.   the mode   d.   the mean

3.   Central tendency is a value that describes a characteristic   **a**
      of scores which are grouped in a:

      a.   frequency distribution
      b.   unequal intervals
      c.   bimodal clusters
      d.   positive categories

4.   The two measures of the form of a frequency distribution are: **d**

      a.   symmetry and asymmetry
      b.   skewness and rectangularity
      c.   triangularity and symmetry
      d.   symmetry and skewness

5.   The clustering of frequency data at different distances from   **b**
      central value is:

      a.   concentration   c.   skewness
      b.   dispersion   d.   kurtosis

6.   The sum of the scores divided by the total number of scores is   **a**
      the definition of the:

      a.   arithmetic mean   c.   median
      b.   mode   d.   weighted mean

7.   For the computation of the mean, the *lowest* level of acceptable   **a**
      measurement is the _____ level.

      a.   interval   c.   nominal
      b.   ratio   d.   ordinal

8.   The distance of each score from the mean of its distribution   **b**
      is the:

      a.   variation   c.   frequency
      b.   deviation   d.   perfumation

9.   The algebraic sum of the mean deviations of all scores is: **b**

      a.   -1   c.   +1
      b.   0   d.   variable

10. The deviations of scores from their mean may be classified as: **c**

   a. weighted or unweighted
   b. affirmative or negative
   c. positive or negative
   d. symmetrical or skewed

11. The grand mean of two or more arithmetic means requires the requires the computation of the _____ mean.   **d**

   a. geometric   c. unweighted
   b. harmonic   d. weighted

12. The score at the 50th percentile of a distribution is the: **c**

   a. average   c. median
   b. mean   d. mode

13. The median is the middle value of a distribution when: **b**

   a. N is an even number
   b. N is an odd number
   c. scores are distributed bimodally
   d. scores are distributed asymmetrically

14. The median is the arithmetic mean of the two middle values when: **a**

   a. N is an even number
   b. N is an odd number
   c. scores are distributed bimodally
   d. scores are distributed asymmetrically

15. To compute the median with several tied scores at the middle values, the best procedure is to convert all scores to: **b**

   a. a grouped frequency distribution
   b. an ungrouped frequency distribution
   c. a bimodal distribution
   d. a histogram

16. For the computation of the median, the *lowest* level of acceptable measurement is the _____level.   **d**

   a. interval   c. nominal
   b. ratio   d. ordinal

17.	The score that occurs with the greatest frequency is the:	**b**

a.	middle value	c.	median
b.	mode	d.	proxy

18.	The sum of all squared deviations around the mean is:	**d**

a.	1	c.	negative
b.	0	d.	minimal

19.	For grouped data, the mode is the _____ of	**c**
the interval containing the highest frequency count.

a.	upper limit	c.	midpoint
b.	lower limit	d.	25th percentile

20.	The mode is represented by the midpoint of the tallest column	**d**
of a (an):

a.	frequency distribution	c.	ogive
b.	frequency polygon	d.	histogram

21.	For the determination of the mode, the *lowest* level of acceptable	**c**
measurement is the _____ level.

a.	interval	c.	nominal
b.	ratio	d.	ordinal

22.	In general, the preferred statistic for central tendency is the:	**a**

a.	arithmetic mean	c.	harmonic mean
b.	median	d.	mode

23.	The median is the preferred measure of central tendency	**c**
for a distribution of scores that is:

a.	normal	c.	skewed
b.	ungrouped	d.	symmetrical

24.	The mean, median, and mode are identical in a	**d**
distribution of scores that is:

a.	grouped	c.	skewed
b.	ungrouped	d.	symmetrical

25. In a positively skewed distribution, the: **b**

    a. median is larger than the mean
    b. mean is larger than the median
    c. mode is larger than the mean
    d. mode is larger than the median

26. For a particular distribution the mode is 68, the median is 62, and   **d**
the mean is 56. This distribution is:

    a. normal   c. positively skewed
    b. symmetrical   d. negatively skewed

27. $N\bar{X}$ is equal to:

                                                                                b

    a. $(X_1 + \bar{X}) + (X_2 + \bar{X}) + ... + (X_n + \bar{X})$
    b. ΣX
    c. $X_1 + X_2 + ... + X_n$
    d. ΣX_3

28. $\Sigma(X - \bar{X})^2$ equals: **d**

    a. the mode
    b. the median
    c. zero
    d. the sum of squared deviations from the mean

29. A group of 20 students obtained a mean score of 70   **b**
on an examination. A second group of 30 obtained a
mean score of 80 on the same examination. The mean score
for the 50 students was:

    a. 70   c. 75
    b. 76   d. 74

30. Which of the following scores is most likely to be the   **c**
median of a positively skewed distribution with a mean
of 65 and a mode of 57?

    a. 40   c. 60
    b. 47   d. 65

31. Which score is most likely to be the median of a negatively   **c**
skewed distribution with a mean of 57 and a mode 65?

    a. 50   c. 60
    b. 57   d. 65

32.   Given that the mean for 60 students is 75 and the mean   **a**
       for 40 women in class is 79, what is the mean for the 20 men?

       a.   67
       b.   71
       c.   75
       d.   77

33.   If the median and the mean are equal, you know that: **a**

       a.   the distribution is symmetrical
       b.   the distribution is skewed
       c.   the distribution is normal
       d.   the mode is at the center of the distribution

34.   If the mean and median are unequal, you know that: **b**

       a.   the distribution is symmetrical
       b.   the distribution is skewed
       c.   the distribution is normal
       d.   the mode is at the center of the distribution

35.   Which measure of central tendency yields the most prosperous   **a**
       picture of income in the United States?

       a.   mean
       b.   mode
       c.   median
       d.   all the same

36.   It is usually possible to see at a glance when looking at a   **c**
       frequency distribution:

       a.   the mean
       b.   the median
       c.   the mode
       d.   all the same

37.   In a bell-shaped distribution of scores: **a**

       a.   the mean, median, and mode are the same
       b.   the mean is usually higher then the median
       c.   the median is usually lower than the mean
       d.   the mean and the median are the same but the mode is
             different

38.   In what type of distribution might the mean be at the 60th   **a**
        percentile?
        a.   positively skewed
        b.   negatively skewed
        c.   normal
        d.   leptokurtic

Computational Problems

An educational sociologist administers an IQ test to a class of college freshman, and she obtains the following hypothetical distribution of scores:

    118, 116, 106, 104, 108, 121, 127, 116, 117,
    114, 123, 109, 115, 129, 127, 115.

1.   Compute the mean IQ of the class.

2.   Compute the median IQ of the class.

3.   Compute the modal IQ of the class.

4.   Describe the skewness of the IQ scores in the class.

An economist compares the annual inflation rates for several Latin American nations and he obtains the following hypothetical distributions of scores:

    9%, 8%, 15%, 22%, 18%, 19%, 25%, 33%, 48%, 11%.

5.   Compute the mean rate of inflation for these countries.

6.   Compute the median rate of inflation for these countries.

7.   Compute the modal rate of inflation for these countries.

8.   Describe the skewness of the inflation rates for these countries.

Answers

1.	116.56	5.	20.8%
2.	116	6.	18.5%
3.	115, 116, 127	7.	no mode
4.	negative	8.	positive

Chapter 6

MEASURES OF DISPERSION

Learning Objectives

After mastering the content of this chapter, you should be able to:

1. *Explain the concept of dispersion and name the five measures of dispersion presented in this chapter.*

2. *Explain the uses and the computation of the range and the interquartile range.*

3. *Explain the uses and computation of the mean deviation.*

4. *Explain the uses and the computation of the variance and the standard deviation.*

5. *Explain how the standard deviation is interpreted.*

Programmed Review

Objective 1. *Explain the concept of dispersion and name the five measures of dispersion presented in this chapter.*

1. The two measures that most fully describe a distribution are the measures of _____ and _____.

central tendency, dispersion

2. A group of scores that clusters closely about its measure of central tendency is a _____ distribution.

homogenous

3. Measures of central tendency and dispersion are necessary for the description of distributions and the interpretation of _____.

individual scores

4. The five measures of dispersion described in Chapter 6 are the _____, the _____, the _____, the _____, and the _____.

range, interquartile range, mean deviation, variance, standard deviation

5. The most useful measure of dispersion for descriptive statistics and basic inferential statistics is the _____.

standard deviation

6. The most useful measure of dispersion for advanced inferential statistics is the _____.

variance

Objective 2. *Explain the uses and the computation of the range and the interquartile range.*

1. An index of variability must indicate a _____ along a scale of scores.

distance

2. The simplest and most straightforward measure of dispersion is the _____.

range

3. The range is the scale distance between the _____ and _____ score.

largest, smallest

4. The range is likely to be distorted by _____.

extreme scores

5. A measure of dispersion that attempts to overcome the instability of the range is the _____.

interquartile range

6. The interquartile range is calculated by subtraction of the score at the _____ percentile from the score at the _____ percentile.

25th, 75th

7. The equation for the interquartile range is _____.

$Q_3 - Q_1$

8. The interquartile range reflects the middle _____ of the scores.

50%

Objective 3. *Explain the uses and computation of the mean deviation.*

1. The sum of the deviations of all scores from the mean is equal to _____.

zero

2. In the computation of the mean deviation, the individual deviations are summed without regard to _____.

sign

3. The mean deviation is based upon the _____ of the deviations.

absolute value

4. The absolute value of a negative number is _____.

positive

5. The absolute value of -17 is _____.

17

6. The symbol for absolute value is _____.

$| \; |$

7. The greater the mean deviation, the greater the _____ of scores. of scores.

dispersion

Objective 4. *Explain the uses and the computation of the variance and the standard deviation.*

1. The sum of the squared deviations from the mean divided by N is the _____.

variance

2. The square root of the variance is the _____.

standard deviation

3. The sum of squares represents the sum of the squared deviation of each score from its _____.

mean

4. When the squared deviations are computed from the mean of the distribution, the value of the sum of squares is _____.

minimal

5. In the computational equation for the standard deviation, the sum of the squared scores is symbolized as _____.

ΣX^2

6. In the computational equation for the standard deviation, the mean squared is symbolized as _____. $\bar{X}^2$

7. In the computational equation for the standard deviation, the standard deviation is symbolized as _____.   **s**

8. In the computation of the standard deviation, the square of the sum of the scores is symbolized as _____. $(\Sigma X)^2$

9. By identification, it is impossible to obtain a sum of squares or a standard deviation that is _____.   **negative**

Objective 5. *Explain how the standard deviation is interpreted.*

1. The size of the standard deviation is directly related to the _____ in the scores.   **variability**

2. The smaller the standard deviation, the more _____ the scores.   **homogenous**

3. The larger the standard deviation, the more _____ the scores.   **heterogeneous**

4. A disproportionate effect on the standard deviation is exerted by _____.   **extreme scores**

5. Complete interpretation of the standard deviation requires knowledge of the relationship between the standard deviation and the _____.   **normal distribution**

Multiple Choice Questions

1. The spread or variability of scores about a measure of central tendency is called: **d**

   a. stratification   c. projection
   b. elongation   d. dispersion

2. The value of a number without regard to sign is called the _____ value.   **a**

   a. absolute   c. natural
   b. relative   d. real

3. The computational equation for the interquartile range is: **b**

   a. $Q^1 - Q^3$ c. $Q^2 - Q^1$
   b. $Q_3 - Q_1$ d. $Q_1 + Q_3$

4. The sum of the deviations of each score from its mean, **b**
   without regard to sign, divided by the number
   of scores is the:

   a. standard deviation c. variance
   b. mean deviation d. semiquartile range

5. The scale distance between the largest and smallest score is the: **a**

   a. range c. semiquartile range
   b. interquartile range d. variance

6. The sum of the squared deviations from the mean, divided by N is the: **c**

   a. standard deviation c. variance
   b. mean deviation d. interquartile range

7. The square root of the variance is the: **b**

   a. mean deviation c. interquartile range
   b. standard deviation d. absolute value

8. The deviations from the mean, squared and then summed is the: **b**

   a. square of the sum c. variance
   b. sum of squares d. standard deviation

9. Which of the following is *not* a measure of dispersion? **c**

   a. the interquartile range c. the median
   b. the mean deviation d. the variance

10. The most useful measure of dispersion for descriptive statistics **c**
    and basic inferential statistics is the:

    a. interquartile range c. standard deviation
    b. mean deviation d. variance

11. The most useful measure of dispersion for advanced inferential **d**
    statistics is the:

    a. interquartile range c. standard deviation
    b. mean deviation d. variance

12.   The most general conception of dispersion is the idea of   **a**
       _____ along a scale of scores.

       a.   distance   c.   time
       b.   speed   d.   area

13.   The simplest and most straightforward measure of distance   **a**
       or dispersion is the:

       a.   range   c.   mean deviation
       b.   interquartile range   d.   standard

14.   The measure of dispersion that is based solely on the two most   **a**
       extreme scores in a distribution is the:

       a.   range   c.   mean deviation
       b.   interquartile range   d.   standard deviation

15.   Compared to the range, the interquartile range is likely to be: **b**

       a.   greater   c.   less stable
       b.   more stable   d.   a negative quantity

16.   The interquartile range is calculated by subtracting the score at the   **c**
       _____ percentile from the score at the _____ percentile.

       a. 15th, 85th c. 25th, 75th
       b. 20th, 80th d. 30th, 70th

17.   Which of the following measures of dispersion enters into   **d**
       the higher mathematical relationships that are basic to inferential
       statistics?

       a.   the range   c.   the mean deviation
       b.   the interquartile range   d.   the variance

18.   The most useful measure of central tendency for normally   **a**
       distributed data is the:

       a.   arithmetic mean   c.   median
       b.   harmonic mean   d.   mode

19.   The sum of the deviations of all scores from the mean divided   **a**
       by N is:

       a.   zero   c.   the variance
       b.   the standard deviation   d.   the interquartile range

20. The sum of the absolute deviations of all scores from the mean divided by N is: **a**

   a. the mean deviation   c. the variance
   b. the standard deviation   d. the interquartile range

21. The absolute value of a negative number is: **b**

   a. a negative number   c. an imaginary number
   b. a positive number   d. zero

22. The symbol for the absolute value of a number is: **c**

   a. ▾   c. | |
   b. #   d. [ ]

23. The measure of dispersion that is based on the squaring of the deviations from the mean is the: **d**

   a. mean deviation   c. absolute deviation
   b. relative deviation   d. standard deviation

24. The sum of the squared deviations from the mean divided by N is the: **c**

   a. standard deviation   c. variance
   b. skew   d. mean

25. The standard deviation is the _____ of the variance.   **b**

   a. square   c. cube
   b. square root   d. cube root

26. The standard deviation is symbolized as: **a**

   a. s c. x
   b. s^2 d. x_2

27. In the text, the sum of the squared deviations from the mean divided by N is called: **a**

   a. the variance   c. the sum of squares
   b. skewness   d. the square of the sum

28. When the deviation of each score is calculated from its mean, the sum of squares is: **c**

   a. zero
   b. negative

   c. minimal
   d. fractional

29. The first term in the computational equation for the standard deviation is the: **b**

   a. square of the sum of the scores
   b. sum of the squares of each of the scores
   c. mean squared
   d. square root of the variance

30. The second term in the computational equation for the standard deviation is the: **c**

   a. square of the sum of the scores
   b. sum of the squares of each of the scores
   c. mean squared
   d. square root of the variance

31. By definition, the standard deviation cannot be a _____ number.   **d**

   a. prime
   b. composite

   c. fractional
   d. negative

32. According to the text, the ratio of the range to the standard deviation usually lies between: **d**

   a. 3 and 4
   b. 4 and 6

   c. 2 and 8
   d. 2 and 6

33. The scores of a distribution with a small standard deviation are referred to as: **c**

   a. normal
   b. symmetrical

   c. homogenous
   d. heterogenous

34. The scores of a distribution with a large standard deviation are referred to as: **d**

   a. normal
   b. symmetrical

   c. homogenous
   d. heterogenous

35. In order to completely interpret the standard deviation,   c
    it is necessary to understand the concept of:

    a.   correlation   c.   the normal distribution
    b.   digression   d.   the frequency distribution

36. Which group of scores exhibits the least variability?   c

    a.   2, 4, 6, 8, 10, 12   c.   2, 6, 7, 7 , 8, 12
    b.   2, 3, 4, 10, 11, 12   d.   2, 2, 3, 11, 12, 12

37. Which groups of scores exhibits the most variability?   d

    a.   2, 4, 6, 8, 10, 12   c.   2, 6, 7, 7, 8, 12,
    b.   2, 3, 4, 10, 11, 12   d.   2, 2, 3, 11, 12, 12

Questions 38 through 41 refer to the following information: The
mean score of 500 students on a statistics test is 45 and the s is 5.

38. If 2 points were added to each of the 500 scores, the new s would be: c

    a.   2.5   c.   5
    b.   3   d.   10

39. If 2 points were subtracted from each of the 500 scores the   c
    new s would be:

    a.   2.5   c.   5
    b.   3   d.   10

40. If each score were doubled, the new s would be: d

    a.   2.5   c.   5
    b.   3   d.   10

41. If each score were divided in half, the new s would be: a

    a.   2.5   c.   5
    b.   3   d.   10

42. Distribution W has a standard deviation of 4. If a score   d
    of 20 has a corresponding z score of -2, what is the mean
    of the distribution?

    a.   12   c.   -12
    b.   -28   d.   28

43. A given distribution has a mean of 60. A score of 75   **a**
has a corresponding z score of +2.00. The standard
deviation is:

    a.   7.5   c.   -12
    b.   -2.00   d.   2.00

44. The standard deviation of the following scores--2, 6, 10--is: **d**

    a.   4   c.   16
    b.   1.63   d.   3.27

45. The variance of the following scores--2, 5, 8, 11--is: **a**

    a.   11.25   c.   214
    b.   15.00   d.   26

46. What is the range of the following scores: 8, 26, 10, 36, 4, 15?   **c**

    a.   7   c.   32
    b.   11   d.   28

Thought Problems

Assume the following distribution of scores: 3, 2, 4, 1, 5.

1. Compute the mean of this distribution.

2. Compute the range of this distribution.

3. Compute the interquartile range of this distribution.

4. Compute the sum of deviations of the scores from the mean.

5. Compute the sum of the absolute deviations of the scores from the mean.

6. Compute the mean deviation for this distribution.

7. Compute the sum of the squared deviations of the scores from the mean.

8. Compute the variance of this distribution.

9. Compute the standard deviation for this distribution.

Assume the following distribution of scores: 1, -3, -1, 3, 5.

10. Compute the mean of this distribution.

11.   Compute the range of this distribution.

12.   Compute the interquartile range of this distribution.

13.   Compute the sum of deviations of the scores from the mean.

14.   Compute the sum of the absolute deviations of the scores from the mean.

15.   Compute the mean deviation of the scores from the mean.

16.   Compute the sum of the squared deviations of the scores from the mean.

17.   Compute the variance of this distribution.

18.   Compute the standard deviation for this distribution.

Computational Problems

A political scientist observes the voter turnout in several counties, and she obtains the following hypothetical rates of voter participation: 45%, 55%, 63%, 78%, 32%, 43%, 42%, 52%, 50%.

1.   Compute the mean rate of voter participation.

2.   Compute the range of voter participation.

3.   Compute the mean deviation of the rates of voter participation.

4.   Compute the variance for the rates of voter participation.

5.   Compute the standard deviation for the rates of voter participation.

A cultural anthropologist observes the child-rearing practices of several African tribes and he obtains the following hypothetical distribution of scores for ratings of child-rearing permissiveness: 78, 42, 83, 41, 76, 82, 55, 68, 79, 60

6.   Compute the mean of the permissiveness scores for all tribes.

7.   Compute the range of the permissiveness scores for all the tribes.

8.   Compute the mean deviation of the permissiveness scores for all the tribes.

9.   Compute the variance of the permissiveness scores for all the tribes.

10.   Compute the standard deviation of the permissiveness scores for all tribes.

Answers

Thought Problems

1.	3	7.	10	13.	0
2.	4	8.	2	14.	12
3.	2	9.	1.41	15.	2.4
4.	0	10.	1	16.	40
5.	6	11.	8	17.	8
6.	1.2	12.	4	18.	2.83

Computational Problems

1.	51.1%	6.	66.4
2.	46%	7.	42
3.	9.68%	8.	13.52
4.	159.21%	9.	231.84
5.	12.62%	10.	15.23

Chapter 7

THE STANDARD DEVIATION AND THE STANDARD NORMAL DISTRIBUTION

Learning Objectives

After mastering the content of this chapter, you should be able to:

1. *Explain the concept of the standard score.*

2. *Describe the basic characteristics of the standard normal distribution.*

3. *Explain how raw scores are converted into z scores.*

4. *Interpret the standard deviation in terms of the normal standard distribution.*

Programmed Review

Objective 1. *Explain the concept of the standard score.*

1.	If scores are to be meaningful, they must be compared to the distribution of scores from some _____.	**reference group**
2.	The deviation of a score from its mean, expressed in standard deviation units, is a _____.	**standard score**
3.	The symbol for designating a standard score is _____.	**z**
4.	In the equation for the transformation of a raw score to a z score, the population mean is referred to as _____.	**mu**
5.	In the equation for the transformation for a raw score to a z score, the population standard deviation is referred to as _____.	**sigma**
6.	A z score represents the deviation of a specific score from the mean expressed in standard deviation _____.	**units**
7.	When the raw score is greater than the mean, the z score is _____.	**positive**
8.	When the raw score is less than the mean, the z score is _____.	**negative**
9.	The sum of z scores equals _____.	**zero**
10.	The mean of z scores equals _____.	**zero**
11.	The standard deviation and the variance of z scores are equal to _____.	**one**
12.	Given a normal distribution of scores, any z score may be expressed as _____.	**percentile rank**
13.	Instead of representing concrete values, z scores represent _____.	**abstract numbers**
14.	Because z scores represent abstract numbers, it is possible to compare an individual's relative position on _____.	**two variables**

Objective 2. *Describe the basic characteristics of the standard normal distribution.*

1.	The population mean of a normal curve is symbolized as _____.	**μ**
2.	The population standard deviation of a normal curve is symbolized as _____.	**σ**

68

3. The mean of all standard normal distributions is _____.   **zero**

4. The standard deviation of all standard normal distributions is _____.   **one**

5. The total area of all standard normal distributions is _____.   **one**

6. The shape of all standard normal distributions is _____.   **symmetrical**

7. In a normal curve, the values of the mean, median, and mode are _____.   **equal**

8. The normal curve never touches the _____.   **X-axis**

9. Because the normal curve never touches the X-axis, it extends _____ in both directions.   **infinitely**

10. In the normal distribution, 68.26% of all cases lie between the mean and _____.   **±1 standard deviation**

11. In the normal distribution, 95.44% of the cases lie between the mean and _____.   **±2 standard deviations**

12. In the normal distribution, 99.74% of the cases lie between the mean and _____.   **±3 standard deviations**

Objective 3. *Explain how raw scores are converted into z scores.*

1. To make use of the normal distribution, the raw scores of a variable must be converted to _____.   **z scores**

2. These z scores may also be called _____ units.   **standard deviation**

3. Given a raw score of 14 on a normally distributed variable with a mean of 16 and a standard deviation of 2, the corresponding z score would be _____.   **-1**

4. According to Table A, the z score of -1 would correspond to a percentile rank of _____.   **15.87**

5. The relationship between z scores and percentile ranks applies only to scores from _____ populations.   **normally distributed**

6. The transformation of raw scores to z scores does *not* alter the shape of the original _____.   **distribution**

7.   If the original distribution of raw scores is nonnormal,   **nonnormal**
      the distribution of z scores will be _____.

Objective 4. *Interpret the standard deviation in terms of the normal standard distribution.*

1.   In a normal distribution, the area between -1 and +1   **68.26%**
      standard deviations includes _____of the cases.

2.   In a normal distribution, the area between -2 and +2 standard   **95.44%**
      deviations includes _____ of the cases.

3.   In a normally distributed population with a mean of 100   **80,120**
      and a standard deviation of 10, one can expect that 95.44%
      of the cases will lie between the scores of _____
      and _____.

Multiple Choice Questions

1.   A z score is the deviation of a specific score from the mean   **c**
      expressed in the units of:

      a.   average deviation   c.   standard deviation
      b.   variance   d.   ranks

2.   When a raw score is greater than the mean, the z score must be: **c**

      a.   fractional   c.   positive
      b.   prime   d.   negative

3.   The z score may also be called a _____ score.   **d**

      a.   regular   c.   percentile
      b.   normal   d.   standard

4.   For any distribution, the sum of the z scores is: **b**

      a.   -1   c.   1
      b.   0   d.   100

5.   For any distribution, the mean of the z scores is: **b**

      a.   -1   c.   1
      b.   0   d.   100

6.   For any distribution, the standard deviation of the z scores is: **c**

    a.   -1   c.   1
    b.   0   d.   100

7.   For any distribution, the variance of the z scores is: **c**

    a.   -1   c.   1
    b.   0   d.   100

8.   For any normally distributed variable, each z score
      will correspond to a: **b**

    a.   measure of association   c.   modal category
    b.   percentile rank   d.   mean rank

9.   The theoretical model that links z scores to percentile ranks is the: **a**

    a.   standard normal distribution
    b.   grouped frequency distribution
    c.   platykurtic distribution
    d.   leptokurtic distribution

10.   The mean of all standard normal distributions is: **b**

    a.   -1   c.   1
    b.   0   d.   100

11.   The standard deviation of all standard normal distributions is: **c**

    a.   -1   c.   1
    b.   0   d.   100

12.   The total area of all standard normal distributions is: **c**

    a.   -1   c.   1
    b.   0   d.   100

13.   The shape of all standard normal distributions is: **b**

    a.   rectangular   c.   asymmetrical
    b.   symmetrical   d.   leptokurtic

14. Which of the following statistics are equal in the standard normal distribution?   **c**

    a.   the mean, standard deviation, and variance
    b.   the first, second, and third quartiles
    c.   the mean, median, and mode
    d.   the mean deviation, standard deviation, and mode

15. The number of cases included in the standard normal distribution is: **d**

    a. N c.   100
    b.   1   d.   infinite

16. For the normal distribution, the area between the mean and -1 standard deviation or +1 standard deviation includes _____ of all cases.   **b**

    a.   29.13%   c.   39.13%
    b.   34.13%   d.   44.13%

17. For the normal distribution, the area between -1 standard deviation and +1 standard deviation includes _____ of all cases.   **c**

    a.   58.26%   c.   68.26%
    b.   63.26%   d.   73.26%

18. For the normal distribution, the area between the mean and 2 standard deviations above or below the mean includes _____ of all cases.   **d**

    a.   32.72%   c.   64.72%
    b.   97.74%   d.   47.72%

19. For the normal distribution, the area between -3 and +3 standard deviations includes _____ of all cases.   **d**

    a.   96.74%   c.   98.74%
    b.   97.74%   d.   99.74%

20. For the normal distribution, the area between -1 standard deviation and +2 standard deviations includes _____ of all cases.   **b**

    a.   76.85%   c.   86.85%
    b.   81.85%   d.   91.85%

21. For the normal distribution, the area between -2 standard   **b**
    deviations and +2 standard deviations includes _____
    of all cases.

    a.   76.85%   c.   86.44%
    b.   95.44%   d.   91.85%

22. According to Table A in the Appendix, a z score of 1.73   **d**
    corresponds to a percentile rank of:

    a.   4.18   c.   92.30
    b.   7.70   d.   95.82

23. According to Table A in the Appendix, a z score of -1.73   **a**
    corresponds to a percentile rank of:

    a.   4.18   c.   92.30
    b.   7.70   d.   95.82

24. If the original distribution of scores is nonnormal, the   **b**
    distribution of z scores will be:

    a.   normal   c.   symmetrical
    b.   nonnormal   d.   rectangular

25. According to Table A in the Appendix, a z score of 1.56   **c**
    corresponds to a percentile rank of:

    a.   90.06   c.   94.06
    b.   92.06   d.   96.06

26. According to Table A in the Appendix, a z score of -0.44   **a**
    corresponds to a percentile rank of:

    a.   33   c.   37
    b.   35   d.   39

27. The fixed point of reference for designating the areas in the normal   **c**
    probability curve is the:

    a.   median   c.   mean
    b.   mode   d.   second quartile

28. To obtain the proportion of the area that lies between   **d**
    two scores on the normal probability curve, it is necessary to:

    a.   add z the scores   c.   compute one z score
    b.   subtract the z scores   d.   compute two z scores

29. For the normal distribution, a z score of +1 corresponds to **b**
    a percentile rank of:

    a. 79.13   c. 89.13
    b. 84.13   d. 94.13

30. For the normal distribution, a z score of 0.5 corresponds to **a**
    a percentile rank of:

    a. 69.15   c. 79.15
    b. 74.15   d. 84.15

31. In the equation for converting a z score to a raw score, **a**
    it is necessary to:

    a. multiply the z score by the standard deviation and add
       the mean
    b. divide the z score by the standard deviation and subtract
       the mean
    c. multiply the z score by the standard deviation and subtract
       the mean
    d. divide the z score by the standard deviation and subtract
       the mean

32. The mean of a normal distribution of scores is 100; $s = 10$. **d**
    The percentage of area between scores 100 and 110 is:

    a. 68.26   c. 50.00
    b. 84.22   d. 34.13

33. If the test scores of 400 students are normally distributed with **b**
    a mean of 100 and σ of 10, the number of students scoring
    between 90 and 110 is:

    a. 136   c. 200
    b. 273   d. 336

34. A statistics professor announces that 15% of the grades he **a**
    gives are As. The results of the final examination indicate
    that the mean score is 83, with a standard deviation of 6.
    What minimum score must a student get to receive an A?

    a. 89   c. 95
    b. 86   d. 92

35. Which *z* score corresponds to the 44th percentile?   **d**

   a.   -1.56   c.   0.15
   b.   -0.44   d.   -0.15

36. Which *z* score corresponds to the 99th percentile?   **c**

   a.   0.99   c.   2.33
   b.   0.49   d.   2.00

37. What percentage of the distribution of scores exceeds   **c**
   a *z* score of 0?

   a.   0%   c.   50%
   b.   25%   d.   100%

38. Assume a raw score of 94; the sample mean is 100.   **d**
   The standard deviation is 3 and $N = 88$. The *z* score is:

   a.   2.0   c.   4.0
   b.   3.0   d.   -2.0

39. Between which *z* score values is the middle 40% of   **b**
   the area under the normal curve included?

   a.   -.25 to .25   c.   -.84 to .84
   b.   -.52 to .52   d.   0 to 1.28

40. You obtain a score of 80 on a test. Which class would   **c**
   you rather be in?

   a.   Mean = 70, $s = 10$ c.   Mean = 60, $s = 15$
   b.   Mean = 75, $s = 5$ d.   Mean = 80, $s = 2$

41. In a normal distribution, approximately what percentage of the cases   **d**
   will fall below a *z* score of 1.00?

   a.   16   c.   66
   b.   34   d.   84

42. In a normal distribution, approximately what percentage of the cases   **a**
   will fall below a *z* score of -1.00?

   a.   16   c.   66
   b.   34   d.   84

43.   A z score is: d

      a.   the deviation from the mean divided by the standard deviation
      b.   the number of standard deviations a score deviates from the mean
      c.   a standard score with a mean of 0.00
      d.   all of the above

Essay Questions

1.   Explain what is meant by the statement that z scores represent abstract numbers as opposed to the concrete values of the original numbers.

2.   If two normal distributions have the same mean, are they identical? Why?

Thought Problems

Assume a normally distributed variable with a mean of 10 and a standard deviation of 4.

1.   Compute the z score for a raw score of 8.

2.   Compute the z score for a raw score of 15.

3.   Compute the z score for a raw score of 10.

4.   Compute the raw score for a z score of 0.75.

5.   Compute the raw score for a z score of -1.5.

6.   State the value of the median for this distribution.

7.   State the value of the mode for this distribution.

8.   State the sum of all z scores for this distribution.

9.   State the mean of all of the z scores for this distribution.

10.   State the standard deviation for all of the z scores in this distribution.

Assume a normally distributed variable with a mean of 100 and a standard deviation of 10. Refer to Table A in the Appendix of the text.

11.   Compute the z score for a raw score of 85.

12.   Compute the raw score for a z score of 0.6.

13.   Compute the percentile rank for a z score of +1.0.

14. Compute the percentile rank for a raw score of 90.

15. Compute the percentile rank for a z score of -1.5.

16. Compute the percentile rank for a raw score of 120.

17. Compute the percent of the distribution that lies between the z scores of -1 and +1.

18. Compute the percent of the distribution that lies between the raw scores of 85 and 115.

19. Compute the percent of the distribution that lies between above a z score of 0.5.

20. Compute the percent of the distribution that lies below a raw score of 85.

21. Compute the z score for the 90th percentile rank of this distribution.

22. Compute the raw score for the 40th percentile rank of this distribution.

Computational Problems

A physical anthropologist measures the height of an entire Amazon tribe, and he finds that the height of the women is normally distributed with a mean of 71 inches and a standard deviation of 5 inches.

1. Compute the z score for a height of 76 inches.

2. Compute the percentile rank for a height of 69 inches.

3. Compute the height at the 30th percentile rank.

4. Compute the height at the 80th percentile rank.

5. Compute the percentage of the distribution that lies between a height of 64 inches and 73 inches.

IQ scores are usually normally distributed with a mean of 100 and standard deviation of 15.

6. Compute the z score for an IQ of 125.

7. Compute the percentile rank for an IQ of 95

8. Compute the IQ at the 90th percentile rank.

9. Compute the IQ at the 20th percentile rank.

10. Compute the percentage of the distribution that lies between an IQ of 93 and 108.

Answers

Essay Questions

1.   The z scores represent the deviations from the mean of the values of any variable expressed in terms of standard deviation units.

2.   It depends on the standard deviations.

Thought Problems

1.	-0.5	7.	10	13.	84.13	19.	30.85
2.	1.25	8.	0	14.	15.87	20.	6.68
3.	0	9.	0	15.	6.68	21.	1.28
4.	13	10.	1	16.	97.72	22.	-0.25
5.	4	11.	-1.5	17.	68.26		
6.	10	12.	106	18.	86.64		

Computational Problems

1.	1	6.	1.67
2.	34.46	7.	37.07
3.	68.4 inches	8.	119.2
4.	75.2 inches	9.	87.4
5.	57.46	10.	38.27

Chapter 8

INTRODUCTION TO CONTINGENCY TABLES

Learning Objectives

After mastering the content of this chapter, you should be able to:

1. *Distinguish between dependent and independent variables in social science research.*

2. *Describe the basic characteristics of bivariate contingency tables.*

3. *Describe the basic techniques of percentaging contingency tables.*

4. *Explain the existence, direction, and strength of statistical relationships.*

5. *Describe the two basic types of measures of association for contingency tables.*

6. *Explain how lambda functions as a nominal measure of association.*

7. *Explain the logical principles of ordinal measures of association.*

8. *Describe Goodman's and Kruskal's gamma as an ordinal measure of association.*

9. *Describe Somer's d as an ordinal measure of association.*

10. *Describe Kendall's tau-b as an ordinal measure of association.*

Programmed Review

Objective 1. *Distinguish between dependent and independent variables in social science research.*

1.	A contingency table is used to analyze _____ simultaneously.	**two variables**
2.	A two-variable analysis is also called a _____ analysis.	**bivariate**
3.	A bivariate analysis normally involves the specification of _____ and _____ variables.	**independent, dependent**
4.	The independent variable is symbolized as _____.	**X**
5.	The dependent variable is symbolized as _____.	**Y**
6.	The independent variable is referred to as the _____ variable.	**predictor**
7.	In an experimental context, the dependent variable is referred to as the _____ variable.	**criterion**
8.	In an experimental context, the independent variable is referred to as the _____ variable.	**experimental**
9.	Whether a variable is designated as an independent variable or a dependent variable is determined by its usage in a specific _____.	**context**

Objective 2. *Describe the basic characteristics of bivariate contingency tables.*

1.	According to conventions for constructing contingency tables, the independent variable is the _____ variable.	**column**
2.	According to conventions for constructing contingency tables, the dependent variable is the _____ variable.	**row**
3.	The separate cells in a contingency table contain the _____.	**cell frequencies**
4.	The column and row totals of the contingency table are referred to as _____.	**marginals**

Objective 3. *Describe the basic techniques of percentaging contingency tables.*

1.	Contingency tables can be percentaged in _____ different ways.	**three**

2. The different techniques for percentaging contingency tables depend on the _____ that is used.

denominator

3. The most common way of percentaging a contingency table is to _____.

percentage down

4. When we percentage down, the denominators for the percentages to be computed are the _____.

column marginals

5. Percentaging down is also referred to as percentaging on the _____.

independent variable

6. Percentaging down permits the determination of the effect of the _____ variable on the _____ variable.

independent, dependent

7. The use of the row marginals as the denominators for the computation of percentages is called _____.

percentaging across

8. When the total number of cases is used as the denominator, the method is called _____.

percentaging on the total

Objective 4. *Explain the existence, direction, and strength of statistical relationships.*

1. The comparison of the percentages within a category of the dependent variable between the two extreme categories of the independent variable is the _____.

percentage difference

2. The percentage difference is also called _____.

epsilon

3. A relationship exists between two variables when none of the epsilons are equal to _____.

zero

4. When higher scores on one variable are consistently associated with lower scores on a second variable, the result is a _____.

negative relationship

5. The strength of a statistical relationship between two variables can range from _____ to _____.

nonexistent, perfect

6. When knowledge of the independent variable does not improve our prediction of the dependent variable, the result is a _____.

nonexistent relationship

7. When knowledge of the independent variable allows complete prediction of the dependent variable, the result is a _____.

perfect relationship

Objective 5. *Describe the two basic types of measures of association for contingency tables.*

1. A measure of association that makes no distinction between the independent and dependent variable is _____ .

    symmetric

2. Symmetric measures of association provide a single summary value of a _____ association.

    two-way

3. An asymmetric measure of association is a summary value of a _____ association.

    one-way

4. A symmetric measure of association requires that the independent and dependent variables are _____ .

    specified

5. The two summary values for asymmetric measures of association result from designating the _____ or _____ variables as independent.

    column, row

Objective 6. *Explain how lambda functions as a nominal measure of association.*

1. Lambda is a statistical measure of association for _____ variables.

    nominal level

2. Lambda is a measure of association that is based on the logic of _____ .

    proportional reduction in error (PRE)

3. In the PRE for lambda, prediction of the dependent variable without knowledge of the independent variable involves _____ .

    Rule I

4. In the PRE for lambda, prediction of the dependent variable with information about the independent variable involves _____ .

    Rule II

5. In the PRE for lambda, the difference in errors between Rule I and Rule II divided by the errors using Rule I equals _____ .

    lambda

6. The value of lambda is the _____ that results upon shifting from prediction Rule I to prediction Rule II.

    proportional reduction in error

7. Lambda measures the _____ of the relationship between two variables.

    strength

8. When knowledge of the independent variable is of no use in predicting the dependent variable, lambda equals _____ .

    zero

9. When knowledge of the independent variable permits perfect prediction of the dependent variable, lambda equals _____.   **one**

10. Since lambda is always positive in sign, it provides no information about the _____ of a relationship.   **direction**

Objective 7. *Explain the logical principals of ordinal measures of association.*

1. The measures of association for contingency tables using ordinal-level data are based on the logic of _____.   **pair-by-pair comparison**

2. The total number of possible pairs in a contingency table is given by the equation_____. $N(N-1)/2$

3. When two cases are ranked in the opposite order on both variables, the result is a _____.   **discordant pair**

4. When two cases are ranked in the same order on both variables, the result is a _____.   **concordant pair**

5. When two cases are ranked similarly on one or both of the two variables the result is a _____.   **tied pair**

6. When discordant pairs predominate, the relationship between the two variables is _____.   **negative**

7. When concordant pairs predominate, the relationship between the variables is _____.   **positive**

Objective 8. *Describe Goodman and Kruskal's gamma as an ordinal measure of association.*

1. A symmetric measure of association for ordinal or interval-level data is _____.   **gamma**

2. The possible values of gamma range from _____ to _____.   **-1, +1**

3. In the equation for symbolizing gamma, *C* represents the number of _____.   **concordant pairs**

4. In the equation for symbolizing gamma, *D* represents the number of _____.   **discordant pairs**

5. Gamma ignores the existence of _____.   **tied pairs**

6. When the concordant pairs outnumber the discordant pairs 3 to 1, the value of gamma will be _____.   **+0.5**

7. The high-high and low-low cells of the independent and dependent variables are connected by the _____.   **positive diagonal**

8. The high-low and low-high cells of the independent and dependent variables are connected by the _____.   **negative diagonal**

9. Gamma is equally useful in predicting the dependent or the independent variable because it is a _____ measure of association.   **symmetric**

10. Because it ignores tied pairs, gamma tends to _____ the strength of the relationship between variables.   **overstate**

11. Gamma is limited to the detection of _____ relationships between variables.   **linear**

Objective 9. *Describe Somer's d as an ordinal measure of association.*

1. An asymmetrical measure of association for ordinal-level data that incorporates tied ranks is _____.   **Somer's *d***

2. In the symbolic equation for Somer's *d*, the number of concordant pairs is _____.   **C**

3. In the symbolic equation for Somer's *d*, the number of discordant pairs is _____.   **D**

4. In the symbolic equation for Somer's *d*, the number of pairs with different *X* values but with the same *Y* values is _____. T_y

5. When calculated for the same contingency table, Somer's *d* must always be less than or equal to _____.   **gamma**

6. Somer's *d* does not have a direct _____ interpretation.   **PRE**

7. Somer's *d* may assume values that range from _____ to _____.   **-1, +1**

Objective 10. *Describe Kendall's tau-b as an ordinal measure of association.*

1. Kendall's tau-*b* differs from Somer's *d* in that its computation involves pairs of cases that are _____.   **tied on both *X* and *Y***

2. Kendall's tau-*b* represents a _____ measure of association for ordinal-level data.   **symmetrical**

3. The maximum value of Kendall's tau-*b* is _____ in a square table.

-1 or +1

4. To compute Kendall's tau-*b* you must first compute _____, _____, _____, and _____.

C, D, T_y, T_x

5. In the computation of Kendall's tau-*b*, T_x equals the number of pairs _____, but with different *Y* values.

tied on *X*

6. Kendall's tau-*b* can never be _____ than gamma due to the incorporation of tied cases in the computation.

larger

Multiple Choice Questions

1. In a two-variable analysis, the variable that is being predicted or explained is the _____ variable.

a

   a. dependent
   b. independent
   c. control
   d. treatment

2. In a two-variable analysis, the variable that serves as the predictor is the _____ variable.

a

   a. independent
   b. dependent
   c. control
   d. criterion

3. The independent and dependent variables are symbolized by the letters:

a

   a. *X* and *Y*
   b. *Y* and *Z*
   c. *A* and *B*
   d. *C* and *D*

4. In an experimental context, the dependent variable is called the _____ variable.

c

   a. experimental
   b. treatment
   c. criterion
   d. input

5. In an experimental context, the independent variable is called the _____ variable.

d

   a. criterion
   b. outcome
   c. control
   d. treatment

6.   In the construction of contingency tables, the independent   **a**
   variable is usually distributed between the:

     a.   columns   c.   positive diagnosis
     b.   rows   d.   negative diagnosis

7.   In the construction of contingency tables, the dependent   **b**
   variable is usually distributed between the:

     a.   columns   c.   positive diagonals
     b.   rows   d.   negative diagonals

8.   The column and row totals of a contingency table are called: **c**

     a.   variable sets   c.   marginals
     b.   ordinals   d.   ratios

9.   A contingency table shows the _____ distribution   **d**
   of two variables.

     a.   absolute   c.   imperative
     b.   relative   d.   conditional

10.   The number of marginals in a 2 x 4 contingency table is: **b**

     a.   four   c.   eight
     b.   six   d.   ten

11.   The number of cells in a 2 x 4 contingency table is: **c**

     a.   four   c.   eight
     b.   six   d.   ten

12.   Which of the following is not one of the three ways   **a**
   of percentaging a contingency table?

     a.   percentaging up   c.   percentaging across
     b.   percentaging down   d.   percentaging on the total

13.   Which of the following is the most common way or percentaging   **b**
   a contingency table?

     a.   percentaging up   c.   percentaging across
     b.   percentaging down   d.   percentaging on the total

14. Which of the following procedures uses column marginals as the base?   **b**

   a.   percentaging up   c.   percentaging across
   b.   percentaging down   d.   percentaging on the total

15. Which of the following procedures uses row marginals as the base?   **c**

   a.   percentaging up   c.   percentaging across
   b.   percentaging down   d.   percentaging total

16. Which of the following is percentaging on the independent variable?   **b**

   a.   percentaging up   c.   percentaging across
   b.   percentaging down   d.   percentaging on the total

17. Which of the following indicates the extent to which the independent variable affects the dependent variable?   **b**

   a.   percentaging up   c.   percentaging across
   b.   percentaging down   d.   percentaging on the total

18. Which of the following procedures uses the total number of cases as the base?   **d**

   a.   percentaging up   c.   percentaging across
   b.   percentaging down   d.   percentaging on the total

19. The comparison of the percentages within the categories of the dependent variable between the two extreme categories of the independent variable results in the: **b**

   a.   proportional reduction in error
   b.   percentage difference
   c.   conditional probability
   d.   coefficient of determination

20. The percentage difference may also be called: **d**

   a.   omicron   c.   theta
   b.   omega   d.   epsilon

21. The statistical relationship between two variables may be classified as either: **c**

   a.   similar or opposite   c.   positive or negative
   b.   affirmative or redundant   d.   assertive or dependent

22. When high scores on one variable tend to be associated with high scores on a second variable, the result is a _____relationship.   **a**

 a. positive   c. curvilinear
 b. negative   d. symmetrical

23. It is impossible to specify the direction of a relationship when one or both of the variables are measured at the _____level.   **a**

 a. nominal   c. interval
 b. ordinal   d. ratio

24. When knowledge of the independent variable fails to improve our prediction of the dependent variable, the result is a _____relationship.   **c**

 a. negative   c. nonexistent
 b. concordant   d. discrepant

25. All measures of association may be classified as either: **c**

 a. abstract or concrete
 b. independent or dependent
 c. symmetric or asymmetric
 d. proportional or relational

26. A single summary value of mutual or two-way association is provided by_____ measures.   **a**

 a. symmetric   c. reciprocal
 b. parallel   d. isomorphic

27. Asymmetric measures of association differ from symmetric measures in that the former require: **c**

 a. more elaborate arithmetic computations
 b. the existence of perfect relationships
 c. the specification of the independent and dependent variable
 d. the transformation of negative relationships to positive relationships

28. Lambda is a measure of association for nominal level variables that is based on the logic of:

    a.   percentage change
    b.   percentaging up
    c.   proportional reduction in error
    d.   concordant and discordant pairs

c

29. In the PRE interpretation, Rule I for lambda assumes:

    a.   complete knowledge of the independent variable
    b.   no knowledge of the independent variable
    c.   no knowledge of the dependent variable
    d.   no knowledge of the level of measurement

b

30. In the PRE interpretation, Rule II for lambda assumes:

    a.   complete knowledge of the independent variable
    b.   no knowledge of the independent variable
    c.   no knowledge of the dependent variable
    d.   no knowledge of the level of measurement

a

31. In the PRE interpretation, lambda is:

    a.   the sum of Rule I and Rule II errors divided by Rule I errors
    b.   the sum of Rule I and Rule II errors multiplied by Rule I errors
    c.   the difference between Rule I and Rule II errors divided by Rule I errors
    d.   the difference between Rule I and Rule II errors multiplied by Rule I errors

c

32. Formally stated, prediction Rule I for lambda is to:

    a.   predict the modal category of the independent variable
    b.   predict the modal category of the dependent variable
    c.   predict the within-category mode of the independent variable
    d.   predict the within-category mode of the dependent variable

b

33. Formally stated, prediction Rule II for lambda is to:

    a.   predict the modal category of the independent variable
    b.   predict the modal category of the dependent variable
    c.   predict the within-category mode of the independent variable
    d.   predict the within-category mode of the dependent variable

c

34. The possible values of lambda range from:　　　　　　　　　　　**b**

   a.　0 to 100　　　　　　　　c.　-1 to 0
   b.　0 to 1　　　　　　　　　d.　-1 to 0

35. When knowledge of the independent variable permits　　　**c**
    perfect prediction of the dependent variable, the value
    of lambda is:

   a.　-1　　　　　　　　　　c.　1
   b.　0　　　　　　　　　　d.　100

36. When all of the within-category modes of the independent　　**b**
    variable occur in the row containing the modal category
    of the dependent variable, lambda equals:

   a.　-1　　　　　　　　　　c.　.5
   b.　0　　　　　　　　　　d.　1

37. Kendall's tau-*b* is:　　　　　　　　　　　　　　　　　**c**

   a.　a symmetric measure of association for nominal level data
   b.　an asymmetric measure of association for nominal level data
   c.　a symmetric measure of association for ordinal level data
   d.　an asymmetric measure of association for ordinal level data

38. The maximum positive value of Kendall's tau-*b* with a square table is:　**a**

   a.　1　　　　　　　　　　c.　100
   b.　-1　　　　　　　　　d.　varies

39. In the computation of Kendall's tau-*b*, T_x is equal to:　　　**c**

   a.　the number of pairs tied on *Y* but with different values of *X*
   b.　the number of pairs tied on *Y* with the same value of *X*
   c.　the number of pairs tied on *X* but with different values of *Y*
   d.　the number of pairs tied on both *X* and *Y*

40. When the number of categories of the dependent variable　　**a**
    exceeds the number of categories of the independent variable,
    tau must be less than:

   a.　1　　　　　　　　　　c.　.25
   b.　.75　　　　　　　　　d.　0

41. Measures of association for contingency tables using ordinal- or interval-level data are based on the logic of:

    c

    a.   nonproportional reduction in error
    b.   simple regression
    c.   pair-by-pair comparison
    d.   magnitude estimation

42. The number of paired comparisons in a contingency table is given by the equation:

    d

    a. N_2 c. $N(N-1)$
    b. N d. $N(N-1)/2$

43. If two cases in a contingency table are ranked in the opposite order on both variables, the result is a _____ pair.

    c

    a.   tied   c.   discordant
    b.   redundant   d.   concordant

44. When two cases in a contingency table are ranked in the same order on both variables, the result is a _____ pair.

    d

    a.   tied   c.   discordant
    b.   redundant   d.   concordant

45. When two cases in a contingency table are ranked similarly on one or both of the variables, the result is a _____ pair.

    a

    a.   tied   c.   discordant
    b.   redundant   d.   concordant

46. When the discordant pairs predominate over the concordant pairs, the relationship between the variables is:

    d

    a.   nonexistent   c.   positive
    b.   curvilinear   d.   negative

47. Goodman's and Kruskal's gamma is:

    c

    a.   a symmetric measure of association for nominal level data
    b.   an asymmetric measure of association for nominal level data
    c.   a symmetric measure or association for ordinal level data
    d.   an asymmetric measure of association for ordinal level data

48. In the equation for the understanding of gamma, the symbol *C* represents: **a**

   a.   the number of concordant pairs
   b.   the number of discordant pairs
   c.   the slope of the positive diagonal
   d.   the slope of the negative diagonal

49. Gamma may assume values ranging from: **a**

   a.   -1 to +1   c.   0 to 100
   b.   0 to +1   d.   -100 to 100

50. In the identification of the discordant pairs of cases, the focal cell lies on the _____ diagonal.   **d**

   a.   absolute   c.   positive
   b.   relative   d.   negative

51. In the computation of gamma, the tied pairs are: **a**

   a.   ignored
   b.   assigned to the concordant pairs
   c.   assigned to the discordant pairs
   d.   evenly divided between the concordant and discordant pairs

52. Somer's *d* is: **d**

   a.   a symmetrical measure of association that ignores tied ranks
   b.   an asymmetrical measure of association that ignores tied ranks
   c.   a symmetrical measure of association that incorporates tied ranks
   d.   an asymmetrical measure of association that incorporates tied ranks

53. When they are computed for the same contingency table: **a**

   a.   Somer's *d* cannot be larger than gamma
   b.   gamma cannot be larger than Somer's *d*
   c.   gamma and Somer's *d* must be equal
   d.   Somer's *d* and gamma must be unequal

54. Somer's d and gamma are based on the assumption of a _____ relationship between variables.   **a**

   a.   linear   c.   *U*-shaped
   b.   nonlinear   d.   curvilinear

Chapter 9

CORRELATION

Learning Objectives

After mastering the content of this chapter, you should be able to:

1. *Explain the concept of correlation.*

2. *Define and explain the calculation of Pearson's r as a coefficient of correlation.*

3. *Explain the relationship between Pearson's r and z scores.*

4. *Explain how the correlation matrix is constructed for several correlation coefficients.*

5. *Explain how correlation coefficients are interpreted.*

6. *Define and explain the computation of Spearman's rho as a coefficient of correlation for ordinal-level data.*

Programmed Review

Objective 1. *Explain the concept of correlation.*

1.   The relationship between two interval or ratio scaled variables
     is described by a measure of association called a _____.   **correlation**
                                                                                 coefficient

2.   The measure of the linear relationship between two
     interval-level variables is _____.   **Pearson's *r***

3.   Pearson's *r* is also called the _____ correlation coefficient.   **product -**
                                                                                 moment

4.   In a scatter diagram, the *X*-axis is the _____ axis.   **horizontal**

5.   In a scatter diagram, the horizontal axis represents   **independent**
     the _____.   **variable**

6.   In a scatter diagram, the vertical axis represents the _____.   **dependent**
                                                                                 variable

7.   In a scatter diagram, the *X*-axis and the *Y*-axis are drawn _____.   **perpendicular**

8.   Each case that appears on scatter diagram represents _____.   **two values**

9.   The values of the Pearson correlation coefficient range   **-1, +1**
     between _____ and _____.

10. The size of the Pearson correlation coefficient indicates   **strength**
     the _____ of the relationship.

11. The direction of a relationship is indicated by the _____   **sign**
     of the correlation coefficient.

12. When high scores on one variable tend to be associated with high   **positive**
     scores on a second variable, the result is a _____ relationship.

13. When high scores on one variable tend to be associated with low   **negative**
     scores on a second variable, the result is a _____
     relationship.

14. A positive relationship may also be called a _____ relationship.   **direct**

15. A negative relationship may also be called an _____ relationship.   **inverse**

Objective 2. *Define and explain the calculation of Pearson's r as a coefficient of correlation.*

1. In the computation of Pearson's *r*, the numerator of the equation represents the _____ of *X* and *Y*.

    covariation

2. The numerator of the computational equation for correlation determines the _____ of the correlation.

    sign

3. The denominator of the computational equation for Pearson's *r* is always _____.

    positive

4. In the raw score equation for the computation of *r*, the first term in the numerator is _____.

    $N \Sigma XY$

5. In the raw score equation for the computation of *r*, the second term in the numerator is _____.

    $(\Sigma X)(\Sigma Y)$

Objective 3. *Explain the relationship between Pearson's r and z scores.*

1. Pearson's *r* can be computed by using _____.

    z scores

2. A high positive *r* indicates that each individual obtains approximately the same *z* score on_____.

    both variables

3. When each individual obtains exactly the same *z* score on both variables, the result is a _____ correlation.

    perfect positive

4. When each individual obtains exactly the same *z* scores of opposite signs, the result is a _____ correlation.

    negative

5. Pearson's *r* represents the extent to which the same individuals occupy the same _____on two variables.

    relative position

6. For a perfect positive correlation, the sum of the products of the paired *z* scores is _____.

    N

Objective 4. *Explain how the correlation matrix is constructed for several correlation coefficients.*

1. A correlation matrix for five variables will contain 10 unique correlation_____.

    coefficients

2. The correlation of a variable with itself is represented on the _____of the correlation matrix.

    diagonal

3.   A correlation matrix with coefficients above and below   **square**
        the diagonal is called a _____.   **matrix**

Objective 5.   *Explain how correlation coefficients are related.*

1.   Pearson's *r* measures the extent of the_____ relationship   **linear**
        between two variables.

2.   For variables with nonlinear relationships, _____   **Pearson's *r***
        should not be computed.

3.   The use of Pearson's *r* assumes that the distributions of both   **unimodal**
        variables are _____ and relatively _____.   **symmetrical**

4.   An artificially low correlation coefficient results when   **restricted**
        the range of one or both variables is _____.

5.   In the interpretation of correlation, a restriction of range may also   **truncated**
        be referred to as _____.   **range**

6.   A correlation may be artificially high when the data set contains   **extreme**
        _____.   **scores**

Objective 6.   *Define and explain the computation of Spearman's rho as a coefficient of*
                   correlation for ordinal-level data.

1.   The symbol for Spearman's rho is _____. r_s

2.   Spearman's rho is used as a measure of correlation for   **ranked data**
        _____ on two variables.

3.   In the computational equation for Spearman's rho, the sum of the ΣD^2
        squared differences is symbolized as _____.

4.   In the computation of Spearman's rho, the number of ranked pairs is   *N*
        symbolized as _____.

5.   The values of Spearman's rho range from _____ to _____.   **-1, +1**

6.   The value of Spearman's rho is +1 when the two sets of ranks are   **agreement**
        in perfect _____.

7.   The value of Spearman's rho is -1 when the two sets of ranks are in   **disagreement**
        perfect _____.

8.   The value of Spearman's rho is artificially inflated by _____.   **tied ranks**

96

9. When there are numerous tied ranks, Spearman's rho should be   **Pearson's *r***
    replaced by _____.

Multiple Choice Questions

1. A measure of association that expresses the extent to
    which two variables are related is the: **b**

    a. z score   c. percentile rank
    b. correlation coefficient   d. standard score

2. The correlation coefficient is used to determine the relationship   **d**
    between two variables measured at the:

    a. nominal or ordinal level
    b. nominal or interval level
    c. ordinal or interval level
    d. interval or ratio level

3. The product-moment correlation coefficient is referred to as: **a**

    a. Pearson's *r*   c. curvilinear
    b. Spearman's rho   d. Somer's *d*

4. Pearson's *r* is a measure of _____ relationship between   **a**
    two variables.

    a. linear   c. curvilinear
    b. nonlinear   d. parabolic

5. The form of the relationship between two interval or   **d**
    ratio level variables is visually represented in a:

    a. pie chart   c. scan chart
    b. pictograph   d. scatter diagram

6. In a scatter diagram, the *X*-axis represents the: **c**

    a. criterion   c. independent variable
    b. control variable   d. dependent variable

7. In a scatter diagram, the *Y*-axis traditionally represents the   **d**

    a. matched variable   c. independent variable
    b. control variable   d. dependent variable

8. In a scatter diagram, the X- and Y-axes are drawn _____ to each other.

    a. parallel   c. perpendicular
    b. diagonal   d. triangular

    c

9. In a scatter diagram, the pairs of X and Y values are called:

    a. parameters   c. coefficients
    b. quartiles   d. observations

    d

10. The values of the Pearson correlation coefficient range from:

    a. 0 to +1   c. 0 to 100
    b. -1 to +1   d. 1 to 100

    b

11. The size of the correlation coefficient indicates the _____ of the relationship between two variables.

    a. strength   c. duration
    b. sign   d. direction

    a

12. The sign of the correlation coefficient indicates the _____ of the relationship between two variables.

    a. strength   c. intensity
    b. duration   d. direction

    d

13. When high scores on one variable tend to be associated with high scores on a second variable, the correlation coefficient describes a _____ relationship.

    a. normal   c. positive
    b. curvilinear   d. negative

    c

14. When high scores on one variable tend to be associated with low scores on a second variable, the correlation coefficient indicates a _____ relationship.

    a. normal   c. positive
    b. curvilinear   d. negative

    d

15. In the mean deviation equation for the calculation of r, the numerator of the equation is called the:

    a. variation   c. standard score
    b. covariation   d. normal score

    b

16. In the mean deviation method for calculating r, the value of the denominator is always: **c**

    a. 1   c. positive
    b. N d. negative

17. The denominator of the equation for the mean deviation calculation of r is always _____ in sign.   **a**

    a. positive   c. neutral
    b. negative   d. cannot predict

18. The Pearson correlation coefficient can also be computed by using: **b**

    a. mean deviations   c. lambdas
    b. z scores   d. gammas

19. In the event of a perfect positive correlation, the z scores of each respondent on each variable are: **d**

    a. reciprocal   c. similar
    b. dissimilar   d. identical

20. In the event of a perfect positive correlation, the sum of the products of the paired z scores is equal to: **d**

    a. 0   c. 1
    b. 1   d. N

21. In the event of zero correlation, the sum of the products of the paired z scores is equal to: **a**

    a. 0   c. 1
    b. 1   d. N

22. The summary table of the statistical relationships between all possible pairs of several variables is a: **c**

    a. scatter diagram   c. correlation matrix
    b. factor loading   d. diagonal pictograph

23. In a correlation matrix, the correlations of each variable with itself are represented on the: **c**

    a. ordinate   c. diagonal
    b. abscissa   d. parallel

24. A correlation matrix with coefficients above and **c**
    below the diagonal is called a _____ matrix.

    a. complete   c. square
    b. rectangular   d. convex

25. According to the text, an *r* of .25 represents a _____ **a**
    relationship.

    a. weak   c. strong
    b. moderate   d. convex

26. According to the text, an *r* of .72 represents a _____ **c**
    relationship.

    a. weak   c. strong
    b. moderate   d. perfect

27. According to the text, a correlation of 1.00 represents **d**
    a _____ relationship.

    a. weak   c. strong
    b. moderate   d. perfect

28. Which of the following is the most important assumption **d**
    of Pearson's *r*?

    a. normal distribution of both variables
    b. similar means for both variables
    c. similar standard deviations for both variables
    d. linear relationship between both variables

29. In order to legitimately use Pearson's *r*, the distributions **b**
    of the two variables must be:

    a. unimodal and perfectly symmetrical
    b. unimodal and relatively symmetrical
    c. bimodal and perfectly symmetrical
    d. bimodal and relatively symmetrical

30. When the respondents are naturally homogenous with respect to a **c**
    particular variable, the Pearson's *r* may be reduced because of:

    a. nonlinearity   c. restriction of range
    b. extreme scores   d. unequal variances

100

31. Pearson's *r* may be artificially high when: c

    a.   there is restriction of range
    b.   the relationship between variables is nonlinear
    c.   the data set contains extreme scores
    d.   the sample is extremely large

32. The measure of correlation that is computed for ranked   c
    data on two variables is:

    a.   Pearson's *r*   c.   Spearman's rho
    b.   lambda   d.   Cramer's phi

33. In the computation of Spearman's rho, the term ΣD b
    must be equal to:

    a.   -1   c.   0 to 100
    b.   0   d.   1 to 100

34. Values of Spearman's rho range from: b

    a.   0 to 1   c.   0 to 100
    b.   -1 to 1   d.   1 to 100

35. When Spearman's rho is equal to one, the two sets of   c
    _____ are in perfect agreement.

    a.   *z* scores   c.   ranks
    b.   percentiles   d.   standard scores

36. The value of Spearman's rho is most likely to be inflated by: c

    a.   restriction of range   c.   tied ranks
    b.   extreme ranks   d.   tied *z* scores

37. When there are numerous ties in the ranked data, the statistic   b
    that should be substituted for Spearman's rho is:

    a.   Somer's *d*   c.   Cramer's *V*
    b.   Pearson's *r*   d.   tau

38. You have correlated the speed of different cars with gasoline   d
    mileage; *r* = 0.35. You later discover that all speedometers
    were set 5 miles per hour too fast. You compute *r*, using
    corrected speed scores. What will the new *r* be?

    a.   -.30   c.   -.07
    b.   -.40   d.   .35

101

39. You have correlated height in feet with weight in ounces; $r = 0.64$. You decide to recompute, after you have divided all weights by 16 to change them to pounds. What will the new r be?   **c**

    a.   .04   c.   .64
    b.   .40   d.   .48

40. For which value of r will the z scores of the X variable be identical to the corresponding z scores on the Y variable?   **c**

    a.   -1.00
    b.   0.00
    c.   1.00
    d.   0.50

41. The correlation between midterm and final grades for 300 students is 0.62. If 5 points are added to each midterm grade, the new r will be: **c**

    a.   .12   c.   .62
    b.   .57   d.   .67

42. When the relationship between two variables is curvilinear, the Pearson's r will be: **d**

    a.   0.00   c.   positive
    b.   negative   d.   low

43. Two variables, X and Y, are to be correlated. The mean of the distribution of scores for the X-variable is 17 and the standard deviation is 0. The r_s will be: **b**

    a.   0.00   c.   -0.50
    b.   0.50   d.   1.00

44. Two variables, X and Y, are to be correlated. The mean of the distribution of scores for the X-variable is 17 and the standard deviation is 0. Pearson's r will be: **a**

    a.   meaningless to calculate   c.   low but positive
    b.   low but negative   d.   1.00

45. For which value of r will the z scores of the X-variable be identical to the corresponding z scores on the Y-variable?   **c**

    a. $r = -1.00$ c. $r = 1.00$
    b. $r = 0.00$ d. $r = .50$

Thought Problems

Assume that the following scores emerged from three observations made on two variables, X and Y.

X	Y	XY	X^2	Y^2
1	2			
2	4			
3	3			

1. Compute ΣX for these scores.

2. Compute ΣY for these scores.

3. Compute ΣXY for these scores.

4. Compute ΣX^2 for these scores.

5. Compute ΣY^2 for these scores.

6. Compute r for these two variables.

7. State the direction of the relationship between these variables.

Assume that the following scores emerged from four observations made on two variables X and Y.

X	Y	XY	X^2	Y^2
1	2			
2	4			
3	2			
4	1			

8. Compute ΣX for these scores.

9. Compute ΣY for these scores.

10. Compute ΣXY for these scores.

11. Compute ΣX^2 for these scores.

12. Compute ΣY^2 for these scores.

13.   Compute *r* for these two variables.

14.   State the direction of the relationship between these variables.

Computational Problem

A sociologist observes the relationship between annual income (*Y*) and number of children (*X*) for 10 families, and she obtains the following scores:

X	Y	XY	X^2	Y^2
0	20K			
0	26K			
1	28K			
1	16K			
2	15K			
2	17K			
3	15K			
4	15K			
4	14K			
6	13K			

1.   Compute ΣX for the these scores.

2.   Compute ΣY for these scores.

3.   Compute ΣXY for these scores.

4.   Compute ΣX^2 for these scores.

5.   Compute ΣY^2 for these scores.

6.   Compute *r* for these scores.

7.   State the direction of the relationship between these variables.

Answers

Thought Problems

1.	6	9.	9
2.	9	10.	20
3.	19	11.	30
4.	14	12.	25
5.	29	13.	-.51
6.	.50	14.	negative
7.	positive		
8.	10		

Computational Problems

1.	23	5.	3445
2.	179	6.	-.71
3.	347	7.	negative
4.	87		

Chapter 10

REGRESSION AND PREDICTION

Learning Objectives

After mastering the content of this chapter, you should be able to:

1. *Explain how correlation is used to predict scores on one variable from knowledge of scores on a second variable.*

2. *Explain the concept of linear regression as a statement of the relationship between two variables.*

3. *Explain the residual variance and the standard error of estimate that result from linear regression.*

4. *Distinguish between the explained and unexplained variation in linear regression.*

5. *Distinguish between correlation and causation in the development of conclusions from findings on prediction and linear regression.*

Programmed Review

Objective 1. *Explain how correlation is used to predict scores on one variable from knowledge of scores on a second variable.*

1. The extent to which the same individuals occupy the same relative position on two variables is measured by _____.

    Pearson's *r*

2. When $r = 0$, our best prediction of an individual's position on the dependent variable is _____.

    $\bar{Y}$

3. When $r = 1.00$, our best prediction of an individual's placement on the dependent variable is _____.

    $z_y = z_x$

4. To completely explain the predictive properties of r, it is necessary to understand the concept of _____.

    linear regression

Objective 2. *Explain the concept of linear regression as a statement of the relationship between two variables.*

1. If one variable occurs earlier in time than another, the earlier variable is designated as the _____.

    independent variable

2. In regression analysis, the independent variable is represented on the _____.

    ***X*-axis**

3. The general algebraic equation for a straight line is _____.

    $Y' = a_y + b_y X$

4. In the equation presented above, the symbol a_y represents a _____.

    constant

5. In the equation presented above, the symbol b_y represents the _____.

    slope of a line

6. The equation presented above may also be referred to as the _____ of Y on X.

    regression

7. In the equation presented above, the symbol a_y represents the value of Y when _____.

    $X = 0$

8. In the equation presented above, the symbol a_y is also referred to as the _____.

    ***Y*-intercept**

9. The Y-intercept is the point at which the regression line crosses the _____.

    ***Y*-axis**

10.	The slope of a regression equation is defined as the _____ of the change in Y to the change in X.	**ratio**
11.	It is possible to compute the slope of a regression line from any two _____ on the line.	**coordinates**
12.	If Y decreases as X increases, the slope of the regression line will be _____.	**negative**
13.	When b = 0, the regression line runs parallel to the _____.	***X*-axis**
14.	In social science research, the correlations obtained are almost never _____.	**perfect**
15.	Due to the absence of perfect correlations, it is necessary to compute a regression equation that provides the _____ to our data.	**best fit**
16.	The best-fitting straight line is defined as the line that minimizes the_____ around it.	**squared deviations**
17.	The best-fitting straight line is referred to as the _____.	**regression line**
18.	In the understanding of regression it is important to note that b_y is equal to _____.	$r \, \dfrac{s_y}{s_x}$
19.	In the equation presented above, the term s_y is the _____ of the Y scores.	**standard deviation**
20.	In the computation of a regression line, the constant a_y is equal to_____.	$\overline{Y} - b_y\overline{X}$
21.	The sum of the deviation of scores around a regression line is _____.	**zero**

Objective 3. *Explain the residual variance and the standard of error of estimates that result from linear regression.*

1.	If $r = 1$, all of the predicted Y scores lie on the _____.	**regression line**
2.	The size and direction of each error in the prediction of each Y score is called a _____.	**residual**
3.	The number of residuals around a regression line will be equal to _____.	***N***

4.	The algebraic sum of the residuals around the regression line is _____.	**zero**
5.	The sum of the squared residuals around a regression line divided by N is the _____.	**residual variance**
6.	The square root of the residual variance is called the _____.	**standard error of estimate**
7.	When $r = \pm 1$, the standard error of estimate is equal to _____.	**zero**
8.	When $r = 0$, the standard error of estimate is equal to _____.	s_y
9.	The smaller the standard error of estimate, the less the _____ of scores around the regression line.	**dispersion**
10.	When the distribution of Y scores for each value of X is normally distributed, the standard error of estimate may be interpreted in terms of the _____.	**normal curve**

Objective 4. *Distinguish between the explained and unexplained variation in linear regression.*

1.	The variation of scores around a sample mean is referred to as the _____variation.	**total**
2.	The total variation may also be called the total _____.	**sum of squares**
3.	The variation of scores around a regression line is referred to as _____.	**unexplained**
4.	Unexplained variation is also called the residual _____.	**sum of squares**
5.	There is no unexplained variation in the event of a _____.	**perfect relationship**
6.	The explained variation is also called the regression _____.	**sum of squares**
7.	It can be shown mathematically that total variation consists of the _____ variation plus the _____ variation.	**unexplained, explained**
8.	When $r = 0$, all of the variation is _____.	**unexplained**

9. When $r = \pm 1$, all of the variation is _____.

   explained

10. The ratio of the explained variation to the total variation is referred to as the _____.

    coefficient of determination

11. The coefficient of determination is symbolized as _____.

    r^2

12. The coefficient of non-determination is symbolized as _____.

    $1 - r^2$

13. When $r = .5$, the coefficient of determination is _____.

    .25

Objective 5. *Distinguish between correlation and causation in the development of conclusions from findings on prediction and linear regression.*

1. The relationship between correlation and prediction frequently leads to the unwarranted assumption of _____.

   causation

2. However, two variables may vary together by virtue of a common link with a _____.

   third variable

3. Causation is especially likely to be inferred when there is a _____ relationship between the two variables under study.

   temporal

4. It is not permitted to infer causation from _____.

   correlation

5. Correlation is a _____ but not a _____ condition to establish causation between two variables.

   necessary, sufficient

Multiple-Choice Questions

1. The measure of association that represents the extent to which the same individuals occupy the same relative position on two interval-level variables is:

   a

   a. Pearson's r c. gamma
   b. Somer's d d. lambda

2. When $r = 0$ our best prediction of an individual's score on the Y variable is:

   a

   a. $\bar{Y}$ c. z_y
   b. X d. z

3. When $r = \pm 1$ our best prediction of an individual's score on the Y variable is: **d**

   a. $\overline{X}$ c. lambda
   b. Y d. z_x

4. Regression analysis is especially useful for problems that require _____ from one variable to another. **b**

   a. explanation   c. extrapolation
   b. prediction   d. experimentation

5. The technique for describing the predictive properties of r is: **d**

   a. magnitude scaling   c. analysis of covariance
   b. limit estimation   d. linear regression

6. In the graphing of a linear regression, it is customary to represent the _____ variable on the X-axis. **b**

   a. dependent   c. criterion
   b. independent   d. concomitant

7. In the general equation for a straight line, the symbol a_y is: **a**

   a. a constant   c. an independent variable
   b. a dependent variable   d. a slope

8. In the general equation for a straight line, the symbol b_y is: **d**

   a. a constant   c. an independent variable
   b. a dependent variable   d. a slope

9. The slope of a line relating values of Y to X is called the _____ of Y on X. **c**

   a. correlation   c. regression
   b. progression   d. suppression

10. The symbol a_y represents the value of Y when X is equal to: **b**

   a. -1   c. 1
   b. 0   d. 100

11. The value of a_y is also referred to as the: **b**

   a. X-intercept   c. solution
   b. Y-intercept   d. slope

12.   The ratio of the change in Y to the change in X is the: **d**

   a. X-intercept   c.   solution
   b. Y-intercept   d.   slope

13.   If Y decreases as X decreases, the value of the slope must be: **a**

   a.   positive   c.   fractional
   b.   negative   d.   greater than 1

14.   When b = 0, the regression line: **a**

   a.   parallels the X-axis
   b.   parallels the Y-axis
   c.   runs perpendicular to the X-axis
   d.   runs diagonal to the X- and Y-axes

15.   The regression line is the line that minimizes the   **a**
       _____ around it.

   a.   squared deviations   c.   skewness
   b.   cross products   d.   mean deviations

16.   When r is equal to b in a regression equation, the: **b**

   a.   means of X and Y are equal
   b.   the standard deviations of X and Y are equal
   c.   means of X and Y are equal
   d.   the standard deviations of X and Y are unequal

17.   The regression line is also referred as the _____line.   **c**

   a.   anticipation   c.   prediction
   b.   expectation   d.   retrodiction

18.   The variance of scores around a regression line is called the: **c**

   a.   total variance   c.   residual variance
   b.   explained variance   d.   prediction variance

19.   The standard deviation of scores around a regression   **c**
       line is called the:

   a. z score
   b.   percentile score
   c.   standard error of estimate
   d.   total variance

20.   The variation of scores around a sample mean of Y is called the: **a**

        a.   total sum of squares
        b.   residual sum of squares
        c.   regression sum of squares
        d.   standard error of estimate

21.   The regression sum of squares is also called the: **c**

        a.   standard error of estimate
        b.   residual sum of squares
        c.   explained variation
        d.   unexplained variation

22.   The ratio of the explained variation to the total variation is   **a**
        symbolized as _____.

        a. r^2 c. d^2
        b. r d. d

23.   The ratio of explained variation to the total variation is called the: **c**

        a.   standard error of estimate
        b.   coefficient of concordance
        c.   coefficient of determination
        d.   coefficient of explanation

24.   When $r = .5$, the coefficient of determination is: **a**

        a.   .25   c.   .71
        b.   -.25   d.   -.71

25.   The proportion of the variation that is *not* explained by the   **c**
        correlation between X and Y is symbolized as:

        a. r^2 c. $1 - r^2$
        b. $r^2 + 1$ d. $1 + r^2$

26.   A correlation between two variables does not warrant   **d**
        the inference of:

        a.   association   c.   regression
        b.   prediction   d.   causation

27.   If the correlation between body weight and annual income were   **d**
       high and positive, we could conclude that:

       a.   high incomes cause people to eat more food
       b.   low incomes cause people to eat less food
       c.   both of the above
       d.   none of the above

28.   The standard error of estimate is used to determine: **d**

       a.   the most probable score for a given individual on a
             predicted variable
       b.   the reliability of a score actually obtained by an individual
             on a test
       c.   the reliability of a coefficient of correlation
       d.   the reliability of a predicted score

Thought Problems

Assume that the scores on two different tests of mental ability are normally distributed with a
mean of 100 and a standard deviation of 15 and that the scores are correlated $r = .70$.

1.   Compute Bob's predicted score on Test 2 if he scores 130 on Test 1.

2.   Compute Mary's predicted score on Test 1 if she scores 80 on Test 2.

3.   Compute Fred's predicted score on Test 1 if he scores 100 on Test 2.

Assume that annual personal income is normally distributed with a mean of $14,000 and a
standard deviation of $5,000. Assume that years of formal education are normally distributed
with a mean of 13 and a standard deviation of 5. Finally, assume that personal income and
formal education are correlated $r = .50$.

4.   Compute Sally's predicted income if she has 18 years of formal education.

5.   Compute Joe's predicted education if he has a personal income of $12,000.

6.   Compute Nina's predicted income if she has 16 years of formal education.

7.   Compute Bill's predicted education if he has a personal income of $7,000.

Computational Problems

Using the provided table, complete the following questions.

	1	2	3	4	5	6	7	8	9	10
Job Satisfaction	10	8	8	5	3	2	0	10	6	4
Age	44	30	35	30	22	37	28	52	40	33

1.   Determine the correlation for the accompanying scores.

Assume job satisfaction is the dependent variable.

2.   Write the regression equation.

3.   Calculate the unexplained, explained and total variation.

4.   Calculate the coefficient of determination.

5.   Calculate the residual and predicted Y value for the first respondent.

Answers

Thought Problems

1. 121

2. 86

3. 100

4. $16,500

5. 12 years

6. $15,500

7. 9.5 years

Computational Problems

1. 0.26

2. $Y' = -3.6288 + 0.2629X_1$

3. 46.38, 58.02, 104.40

4. 0.44

5. 2.06, 7.94

Chapter 11

MULTIVARIATE DATA ANALYSIS

Learning Objectives

After mastering the content of this chapter, you should be able to:

1. *Explain the uses of multivariate statistical techniques.*

2. *Explain the construction and analysis of multivariate contingency tables.*

3. *Explain the uses and computation of partial correlation as a technique of multivariate data analysis.*

4. *Explain the uses and computation of multiple regression as a technique of multivariate data analysis.*

Programmed Review

Objective 1. *Explain the uses of multivariate statistical techniques.*

1.	The procedures for the simultaneous analysis of three or more variables are called _____ techniques.	**multivariate statistical**
2.	The three multivariate statistical techniques presented in this chapter are_____ analysis, _____ analysis, and _____ analysis.	**contingency table, partial correlation, multiple regression**

Objective 2. *Explain the construction and analysis of multivariate contingency tables.*

1.	Conditional tables summarize the relationship between _____ for subgroups, categories, or conditions of one or more additional variables.	**two variables**
2.	A third variable in a conditional table is called the _____ variable.	**control (test)**
3.	The control or test variable in a conditional table is designated by the letter _____.	Z
4.	The introduction of a control or test variable into an analysis is called _____.	**statistical elaboration**
5.	The number of control or test variables determines the _____ of a conditional table.	**order**
6.	In the statistical elaboration of a nominal-level variable, the effect of the test variable can be eliminated by _____.	**physical control**
7.	In the statistical elaboration of an ordinal- or interval-level variable, the effect of the test variable is _____ but not eliminated.	**reduced**
8.	The variation within an ordinally or intervally measured variable can be reduced by increasing the number of _____.	**categories**

Objective 3. *Explain the uses and computation of partial correlation as a technique of multivariable data analysis.*

1.	A measure of the linear relationship between two interval-level variables, controlling for one or more additional variables, is a _____.	**partial correlation coefficient**

2. The control procedure used with multivariate contingency tables is _____, but the control procedure used in partial correlation analysis is _____.

physical, statistical

3. In the equation for the computation of partial correlation, the control variable is symbolized as _____.

Z

4. A partial correlation coefficient may be defined as a weighted average of the _____ correlations between two variables within categories of the control variable.

zero-order

5. If the partial correlation coefficient is to be a useful tool, the zero-order association between variables should be generally uniform across all categories of the _____.

control variable

Objective 4. *Explain the uses and computation of multiple regression as a technique of multivariate data analysis.*

1. A logical extension of simple regression is _____.

multiple regression

2. Multiple regression employs two or more _____.

independent variables

3. Two or more independent variables in a multiple regression serve as _____ of a dependent variable.

predictors

4. In the generalized equation for multiple regression with independent variables, the predicted value of the dependent variable is symbolized as _____.

Y'

5. In the generalized equation for multiple regression with two independent variables, the Y-intercept is symbolized as _____.

a_y

6. In the generalized equation for multiple regression with two independent variables, the slope associated with the second independent variable is symbolized as _____.

b_2

7. In the illustration of multiple regression with two independent variables, the best fit to the scores is a _____.

regression plane

8. In multiple regression, the tilt of the regression plane is determined by the values of the _____.

slopes

9. In multiple regression, the point at which the regression plane crosses the Y-axis is symbolized as _____.

    a_y

10. The measure of the influence of an independent variable on a dependent variable when the effects of all other independent variables in the multiple regression equation have been held constant is the _____.

    multiple regression coefficient

11. It is possible to assess the relative importance of each independent variable in multiple regression with_____.

    standardized regression coefficients

12. Standardized regression coefficients are symbolized as _____.

    β

13. To convert unstandardized regression coefficients into standardized coefficients, it is necessary to compute the _____ of the independent and dependent variables.

    standard deviations

14. The measure of the linear relationship between a dependent variable and the combined effects of two or more independent variables is the _____.

    multiple correlation coefficient

15. The multiple correlation coefficient is symbolized as _____.

    R

16. The squaring of *R* yields the coefficient of _____.

    multiple determination

Multiple Choice Questions

1. A variable that casually links two other variabies is _____variable.

    c

    a. an independent   c. an intervening
    b. a dependent   d. a test

2. A control variable is the same as _____ variable.

    d

    a. an independent   c. an interviewing
    b. a dependent   d. a test

3. The relationships between three or more variables are analyzed with:

    b

    a. scatter diagrams
    b. multivariate statistical techniques
    c. zero-order correlations
    d. spectographic examinations

4. The relationships between two variables for subgroups,   **c**
    categories, or conditions of one or more additional
    variables are summarized with:

    a.   square root tables   c.   conditional tables
    b.   random number tables   d.   normal tables

5. Conditional tables are also called: **c**
    a.   control tables   c.   partial tables
    b.   test tables   d.   normal tables

6. A variable whose subgroups or categories are used   **a**
    in a conditional table to examine the relationship
    between two variables is a:

    a.   control variable   c.   partial variable
    b.   intervening variable   d.   spurious variable

7. A control variable is also called a: **d**

    a.   partial variable   c.   intervening variable
    b.   conditional variable   d.   test variable

8. The introduction of a control or test variable into a   **b**
    two-variable analysis is called:

    a.   multiple causation   c.   bivariate analysis
    b.   statistical elaboration   d.   qualitative analysis

9. The number of control or test variables determines the   **d**
    _____ of a conditional table.

    a.   priority   c.   articulation
    b.   elaboration   d.   order

10. The effects of a nominal-level test variable are eliminated through: **a**

    a.   physical control   c.   logical control
    b.   statistical control   d.   operant control

11. The variation within the categories of an ordinally or intervally   **a**
    measured test variable can be reduced by:

    a.   increasing the number of categories
    b.   decreasing the number of categories
    c.   increasing *N*
    d.   decreasing *N*

12. When two variables are correlated because of their common association with a third variable, the result is a: **b**

   a. partial correlation
   b. spurious relationship
   c. pseudo effect
   d. conditional outcome

13. The measure of the linear relationship between two interval-variables, controlling for one or more additional variables, is a: **a**

   a. partial correlation
   b. point correlation
   c. multiple correlation
   d. contention correlation

14. Compared to the concept of physical control used with multivariate contingency tables, the procedure used in partial correlation is called: **c**

   a. rational control
   b. empirical control
   c. statistical control
   d. descriptive

15. In the partial correlation coefficient, the control variable is symbolized as: **d**

   a. A
   b. B
   c. T
   d. Z

16. The values of partial correlation coefficients may range from: **b**

   a. 0 to +1.0
   b. -1.0 to +1.0
   c. 0 to 100
   d. -1.0 to 100

17. When the relationship between X and Y is not uniform across all categories of the control variable, the partial correlation coefficient should be replaced by a **b**

   a. multiple regression equation
   b. multivariate contingency table
   c. gamma
   d. lambda

18. In a multiple regression equation with two or more independent variables, the predicted value of the dependent variable is symbolized as: **d**

   a. a_y
   b. b_1
   c. b_2
   d. Y'

19. In a multiple regression equation with two or more independent variables, the Y-intercept is symbolized as: **a**

    a. a_y c. b_2
    b. b_1 d. Y'

20. In a multiple regression equation with two independent variables, the slope associated with the second independent variable is symbolized as: **c**

    a. a_y c. b_2
    b. b_1 d. Y'

21. In a multiple regression analysis with two independent variables, the structure of best fit is called the: **c**

    a. regression point   c. regression plane
    b. regression line   d. regression sphere

22. In a multiple regression equation, the values immediately preceding X_1 and X_2 are called multiple regression: **a**

    a. coefficients   c. predictors
    b. correlations   d. indicators

23. In order to assess the relative importance of each independent variable as a predictor of the dependent variable, it is necessary to use _____ regression coefficients.   **c**

    a. normalized   c. standardized
    b. studentized   d. customized

24. Standardized regression coefficients are symbolized as: **b**

    a. α   c. φ
    b. β   d. ó

25. To convert an unstandardized regression coefficient for X to a standardized regression coefficient it is necessary to first: **d**

    a. add the standard deviation of X_1 and Y
    b. multiply the standard deviations of X_1 and Y
    c. subtract the standard deviation of X_1 from the standard deviation of Y
    d. divide the standard deviation of X_1 by the standard deviation of Y

26. A measure of the linear relationship between a dependent variable   **a**
    and the combined effects of two or more independent variables is
    the:

    a. multiple correlation coefficient
    b. multiple regression coefficient
    c. partial correlation coefficient
    d. partial regression coefficient

27. The multiple correlation coefficient is symbolized as: **c**

    a. A c. R
    b. B d. Z

28. The proportion of the total variation in a dependent variable   **c**
    that is jointly explained by two or more independent variables is
    the:

    a. standard error of estimate
    b. residual sum of squares
    c. coefficient of multiple determination
    d. standardized regression coefficient

Computational Problems

Using the provided table, complete the following questions.

	1	2	3	4	5	6	7	8	9	10
Job Satisfaction	10	8	8	5	3	2	0	10	6	4
Age	44	30	35	30	22	37	28	52	40	33
Years Worked	22	7	8	10	1	15	6	30	20	12

Assume job satisfaction is the dependent variable.

$Y' = -13.4359 + 0.7127$ Age $- 0.4566$ Years Worked

TSS = 104.40, RSS = 50.54, and RegSS = 53.86

1. Calculate the coefficient of determination.

2. Calculate the coefficient of non-determination.

3. Calculate the residual and predicted Y value for the first respondent.

Answers

1.   0.52   2.   0.48   3.   2.12, 7.88

Chapter 12

PROBABILITY

Learning Objectives

After mastering the content of this chapter, you should be able to:

1. *Explain the concepts of probability and randomness.*

2. *Describe the basic approaches to the understanding of probability.*

3. *Describe the most important formal rules for understanding and computing probability.*

4. *Explain the rules of probability for continuous variables.*

5. *Distinguish between one-tailed and two-tailed probability values.*

Programmed Review

Objective 1. *Explain the concepts of probability and randomness.*

1.	At the most elementary level, probability may be understood as the _____ of occurrence for any event.	**likelihood**
2.	An important technique for selecting a representative sample from a population is _____.	**simple random sampling**
3.	A sampling procedure in which one element of a population is more likely to be selected than another element is called _____.	**biased**
4.	It is dangerous to generalize from a biased sample to a _____.	**population**
5.	The statistical tests presented in the text require _____ random sampling.	**independent**
6.	Two events are independent if the selection of one has no effect upon the _____ of selecting the second.	**probability**
7.	A commonly used technique of random sampling is a table of _____.	**random numbers**

Objective 2. *Describe the basic approaches to the understanding of probability.*

1.	The theory that is concerned with the possible outcomes of a study is _____.	**probability**
2.	To compute a probability, it must be possible to list each _____ that can occur.	**outcome**
3.	You must then be able to state the _____ of these outcomes.	**expected relative frequencies**
4.	The two general approaches to probability theory are the _____ and _____.	**classical, empirical**
5.	The theory of probability has always been closely associated with _____.	**games of chance**

6.	In the classical definition of probability, the number of outcomes in which event *A* occurs is divided by the _____ of outcomes of event *A*.	**total number**
7.	In the classical definition, probability is defined as a _____.	**proportion**
8.	In the classical definition of probability, the composition of the _____ is known.	**population**
9.	In real life situations, the expected relative frequencies are assigned on the basis of _____.	**empirical findings**

Objective 3. *Describe the most important formal rules for understanding and computing probability.*

1.	In the classical definition, probability is symbolized as _____.	***p***
2.	The value of *p* may range between _____.	**0 and 1**
3.	If an event is certain to occur, its probability is _____.	**1**
4.	When probability is expressed as the number of chances in 100, the result is a _____.	**percentage**
5.	Probability may also be expressed as the _____ the occurrence of the events.	**odds against**
6.	If a probability is equal to .1, the odds against the occurrence of the event are _____.	**9 to 1**
7.	The probability of *A* plus the probability of *B* minus the probability of their joint occurrence is the probability of obtaining either *A* or *B*. This statement is the _____.	**addition rule**
8.	According to the addition rule, the probability of drawing either an ace or a heart from a standard deck of 52 cards is _____.	**4/13**
9.	If both events *cannot* occur simultaneously, then *A* and *B* are _____.	**mutually exclusive**
10.	The addition rule for two mutually exclusive events is $p(A \text{ or } B) =$ _____.	***p(A)* + *p(B)***
11.	In probabilities for problems based on dichotomous, yes/no, or two-category variables, the events under study are mutually exclusive and _____.	**exhaustive**

12. In the case of mutually exclusive and exhaustive events, the probability of event *A* and the probability of event *B* is equal to _____.

1

13. In the treatment of dichotomous populations, it is common to symbolize the probability of the *occurrence* of an event as _____.

P

14. In the treatment of dichotomous populations, it is common to symbolize the probability of the *nonoccurrence* of an event as _____.

Q

15. When the events are mutually exclusive and exhaustive, the value of *Q* is equal to _____.

1 - P

16. When more than one draw or trial is involved in a probability problem, it is necessary to determine the probability of the _____ of two or more events.

successive occurrence

17. The probability of the successive occurrences of two events is the product of the separate probabilities of each event. This statement is the _____.

multiplication rule

18. Following the multiplication rule, the probability of events *A* and *B* is symbolized as _____.

p(A) p(B)

19. In the use of the multiplication rule, if the events are sampled with replacement, they are _____.

independent

20. The probability of obtaining both *A* and *B* jointly is the product of the probability of obtaining one of these events times the conditional probability of obtaining one event, given that the other event has occurred. This statement is the multiplication rule for _____.

dependent events

21. The probability of *B* given that *A* has occurred is symbolized as _____.

p(B|A)

22. The probability of *B* given that *A* has occurred is called a _____.

conditional probability

Objective 4. *Explain the rules of probability for continuous variables.*

1. At this point, probability has been defined in terms of the _____ of an event.

expected relative frequency

2. The relative frequency definition of probability presents a problem when we are dealing with _____.

continuous variables

3. For continuous variables, probability may be expressed as the area under portions of a curve divided by the _____ under the curve.   **total area**

4. The total area in a continuous probability distribution is equal to _____.   **1**

Objective 5. *Distinguish between one-tailed and two tailed probability values.*

1. The standard normal distribution has a mean of _____.   **0**

2. The standard normal distribution has a standard deviation of _____.   **1**

3. The standard normal distribution has a total area that is equal to _____.   **1**

4. The proportions of total area under the normal curve establish _____.   **probability values**

5. The probability value that results from examining only one tail of a distribution is a _____.   **one-tailed *p* value**

6. The probability value that results from examining both tails of a distribution is a _____.   **two-tailed *p* value**

7. A two-tailed *p* value may be obtained from the one-tailed *p* value if the distribution is _____.   **symmetrical**

8. The distinction between one- and two-tailed probability values is most significant for the understanding of _____.   **inferential statistics**

Multiple-Choice Questions

1. In everyday life people make judgements based on the _____ use of probability.   **c**

   a.   formal   c.   intuitive
   b.   logical   d.   scientific

2. The intuitive probabilities that are used in everyday life are most similar to the general idea of: **b**

   a.   randomness   c.   normality
   b.   likelihood   d.   sampling

3.   In most cases, population parameters are estimated from: **a**

  a.   sample statistics   c.   sampling with replacement
  b.   biased samples   d.   sampling without replacement

4.   When each member of a sample has the same probability   **b**
      of being selected, the procedure is called:

  a.   biased sampling   c.   sampling with replacement
  b.   simple random sampling   d.   sampling without replacement

5.   If the selection of one event has no effect upon the probability   **c**
      of selecting a second event, the two events are said to be:

  a.   unique   c.   independent
  b.   dependent   d.   unrelated

6.   If any element of a sample is more likely to be selected than another   **b**
      element, the result is:

  a.   simple random sampling   c.   sampling with replacement
  b.   biased sampling   d.   sampling without replacement

7.   The inferential statistical tests presented in this text require: **b**

  a.   dependent random sampling
  b.   independent random sampling
  c.   dependent biased sampling
  d.   independent biased sampling

8.   The development of probability theory and the understanding   **c**
      of independent sampling has been closely associated with:

  a.   the development of computers
  b.   musical notation
  c.   games of chance
  d.   political

9.   The theory that is concerned with the possible outcomes of a study   **b**
      is called:

  a.   predictability   c.   reliability
  b.   probability   d.   repeatability

10. The number of outcomes in which event A occurs divided by the total number of outcomes is the _____ definition of probability.   **b**

   a. rational   c. empirical
   b. classical   d. psychological

11. According to the classical definition, probability is defined as a: **c**

   a. percentage   c. proportion
   b. percentage change   d. percentile

12. In the classical definition of probability, the: **a**

   a. population characteristics are known.
   b. population characteristics are estimated.
   c. sample characteristics are estimated.
   d. number of possible outcomes is unknown.

13. In the empirical definition of probability, the: **b**

   a. population characteristics are known.
   b. population characteristics are estimated.
   c. sample characteristics are estimated.
   d. number of possible outcomes is unknown.

14. In the definition of probability, the value of p ranges from _____ to _____.   **b**

   a. -1 to 1   c. 0 to 100
   b. 0 to 1   d. -0 to 100

15. A probability statement that is expressed as a number of chances in 100 is a: **b**

   a. ratio   c. percentage change
   b. percentage   d. proportion

16. If the probability of event A is .02, then the odds against the occurrence of event A are: **d**

   a. 19 to 1   c. 39 to 1
   b. 29 to 1   d. 49 to 1

17.	The two arithmetic rules of probability described in the text		c
	are the:

	a.	addition rule and subtraction rule
	b.	multiplication rule and division rule
	c.	addition rule and multiplication rule
	d.	subtraction rule and division rule

18.	The addition rule states the probability of obtaining:		a

	a.	either of two events
	b.	both of two events
	c.	the successive occurrence of events
	d.	one event given that the second event has occurred

19.	The multiplication rule states the probability of obtaining:		c

	a.	either of two events
	b.	both of two events
	c.	the successive occurrence of events
	d.	one event given that the second event has occurred

20.	If two events cannot occur simultaneously, they are:		b

	a.	exhaustive			c.	mutually
	b.	mutually exclusive		d.	reciprocal

21.	According to probability theory, events that are based		b
	on dichotomous or two-category variables are:

	a.	reciprocal			c.	mutually
	b.	exhaustive			d.	normally distributed

22.	In a dichotomous population, the probability of the		b
	occurrence of an event is symbolized as:

	a.	N				c.	Q
	b.	P				d.	Z

23.	In a dichotomous population, the probability of the		c
	nonoccurrence of an event is symbolized as:

	a.	N				c.	Q
	b.	P				d.	Z

24. When the events are mutually exclusive and exhaustive, the sum of *P* and *Q* is equal to: **c**

   a.   -1.0   c.   1.0
   b.   0   d.   100

25. When sampling with replacement, the events are classified as: **a**

   a.   independent   c.   conditional
   b.   dependent   d.   related

26. When sampling without replacement, events are classified as: **c**

   a.   random   c.   dependent
   b.   improbable   d.   uncorrelated

27. The probability of *A* given that *B* has occurred is: **c**

   a.   a relative probability   c.   a conditional probability
   b.   an independent probability   d.   a contingent probability

28. In dealing with continuous variables, probability is best expressed as: **c**

   a.   an expected relative frequency
   b.   a slice in a pie chart
   c.   a portion of a curve
   d.   a projection on a trend chart

29. When probability is expressed as the area under portions of a curve, it is most useful if the curve approximates: **a**

   a.   a normal distribution   c.   a leptokurtic distribution
   b.   a platykurtic distribution d.   an ogive

30. A probability value that takes account of both ends of the normal distribution is: **c**

   a.   multivariate   c.   two-tailed
   b.   leptokurtic   d.   reciprocal

31. The distinction between one- and two-tailed probability values is of most significance in the study of: **d**

   a.   measures of central tendency
   b.   measures of dispersion
   c.   multiple regression
   d.   inferential statistics

32. If the probability that an event will occur is .10, the odds against this event occurring are: **c**

    a.   10 to 1   c.   9 to 1
    b.   1 to 10   d.   1 to 9

33. If the odds in favor of an event occurring are 7 to 1, the probability of this event occurring is: **d**

    a.   1/7   c.   6/7
    b.   1/6   d.   7/8

34. If one card is selected from a well-shuffled 52-card deck of playing cards, the probability of obtaining a five is: **c**

    a.   5/52   c.   1/13
    b.   1/12   d.   5/47

35. The odds against drawing a heart from a well-shuffled 52-card deck of playing cards are: **d**

    a.   13 to 1   c.   12 to 1
    b.   4 to 1   d.   3 to 1

36. We toss a pair of dice. The probability of obtaining a 5 on the first die and a 6 on the second die is: **d**

    a.   1/6   c.   1/35
    b.   1/3   d.   1/36

37. Sampling with replacement: Two cards are drawn from a 52-card deck of playing cards. The probability of selecting a heart and a king is: **a**

    a.   52/2704   c.   16/52
    b.   39/2704   d.   52/2605

38. Given $\mu = 50$, $\sigma = 5$, the probability of selecting at random an individual with a score of 40 or less is: **d**

    a.   .45   c.   .48
    b.   .05   d.   none of the above

39. Given $\mu = 20$, $\sigma = 2$, the probability of selecting at random an individual with a score as rare or unusual as 17 is: **d**

    a.   .93   c.   .87
    b.   .07   d.   .13

138

40. On the basis of chance, the probability of obtaining a case which   **b**
    falls between $z = -.50$ and $z = -1.00$ under the normal curve is:

    a.   5 in a hundred   b.   20 in a hundred
    b.   15 in a hundred   c.   34 in a hundred

41. Bill Clinton tosses a pair of dice. The probability that the sum will   **a**
    be an odd number and that a four will appear on at least one die is:

    a.   1/6   c.   18/36
    b.   5/36   d.   1/9

42. Mutually exclusive events are: **d**

    a.   never independent   c.   dependent
    b.   always related   d.   none of the above

Thought Problems

Assume four tosses of an unbiased coin.

1. Compute the probability of obtaining four heads.

2. Compute the probability of obtaining three heads.

3. Compute the probability of obtaining two heads.

4. Compute the probability of obtaining one head.

5. Compute the probability of obtaining no heads.

Assume drawing with replacement from a 52 card deck.

6. Compute the probability of drawing two diamonds.

7. Compute the probability of drawing a seven or a spade.

8. Compute the probability of drawing a two aces.

9. Compute the probability of drawing a spade, a diamond, a nine, or four.

State each of the following probabilities as odds.

10. .1

11. .2

12. .05

13. .4

Answers

1.	.0625	5.	.0625	9.	.58	13.	3 to 2
2.	.25	6.	.0625	10.	9 to 1		
3.	.375	7.	.31	11.	4 to 1		
4.	.25	8.	.0059	12.	19 to 1		

Chapter 13

INTRODUCTION TO STATISTICAL INFERENCE

Learning Objectives

After mastering the content of this chapter, you should be able to:

1. *Explain why sampling is necessary for the inference of population parameters.*

2. *Explain the origins of a sampling distribution for statistics.*

3. *Explain how the binomial distribution approximates the normal distribution.*

4. *Explain the level of significance in the testing of statistical hypotheses.*

5. *Explain the use of the null hypothesis and the alternative hypothesis in the testing of statistical hypotheses.*

6. *Explain the two types of errors that must be considered in the testing of statistical hypotheses.*

7. *Explain some of the precautions that are necessary in the interpretation of statistical tests.*

Programmed Review

Objective 1. *Explain why sampling is necessary for the inference of population parameters.*

1. A complete or theoretical set of individuals, objects, or **population** measurements having some common observable characteristic is a _____.

2. The measurable characteristics of a population are its _____. **parameters**

3. Testing hypotheses about population parameters **sample** involve_____. **statistics**

4. Sample statistics for are used to make _____ about **inferences** population parameters.

Objective 2. *Explain the origins of a sampling distribution for a statistic.*

1. Inferences about the parameters of populations are made from **N** statistics that are calculated from a sample of _____. **observations**

2. The observations of a sample are drawn _____ from **at random** the population.

3. The result of drawing all possible samples of a fixed size from **sampling** a given population is a _____.

    distribution

4. A sampling distribution is a theoretical probability distribution of **sample** the possible values of a _____. **statistic**

5. Description of the sampling distribution of a statistic permits **hypotheses** the testing of _____.

6. The description of the form of a sampling distribution requires **models** the use of idealized _____.

7. Two models that are frequently used to describe particular **normal** **curve,** sampling distributions are the _____ and _____. **binomial** **distribution**

Objective 3. *Explain how the binomial distribution approximates the normal distribution.*

1. The true proportion of heads and tails characterizing a **unknowable** coin is _____.

2. This population parameter is unknowable because it is based on an _____ number of outcomes. **infinite**

3. The estimation of the parameter of heads and tails for the coin depends on _____. **sampling**

4. The hypothesis that the coin is unbiased is symbolized as _____. **$P = Q = \frac{1}{2}$**

5. The hypotheses that the coin is biased is symbolized a _____. **$P \neq Q \neq \frac{1}{2}$**

6. The probability of obtaining one head and one tail in two tosses of an unbiased coin is _____. **.5**

7. When P and Q approximate $\frac{1}{2}$, and N is large, the shape of the binomial distribution approximates the _____. **normal distribution**

8. The normal distribution is a model for a sampling distribution with_____. **continuous variables**

9. The binomial distribution is a model for a sampling distribution with _____. **dichotomous variables**

Objective 4. *Explain the level of significance in the testing of statistical hypotheses.*

1. The probability of obtaining exactly 5 heads and 5 tails in 10 tosses of an unbiased coin is _____. **.246**

2. The basis for inferring the operation of nonchance factors in any particular statistical finding is the _____. **cutoff point**

3. The two cutoff points preferred by most social science researchers are the .05 and .01_____. **significance levels**

4. The .05 significance level states that a particular finding would occur by chance _____ of the time or less. **5%**

5. The .01 significance level states that a particular finding would occur by chance _____of the time or less. **1%**

6. The significance level set by researchers for inferring the operation of nonchance factors is called the _____. **alpha level**

7. The probability of an event as rare as nine heads in ten tosses of an unbiased coin is _____. **.010**

8.	Given a significance level of .05 and finding of nine heads in ten tosses, we would conclude that the coin was_____.	**biased**
9.	Given a .01 significance level and nine heads from ten tosses, we could not reject the hypothesis that the coin was _____.	**unbiased**
10.	The alpha level must be specified before the execution of the _____.	**study**

Objective 5. *Explain the use of the null hypothesis and the alternative hypothesis in the testing of statistical hypotheses.*

1.	Prior to the beginning of any study, the research sets up two mutually exclusive _____.	**hypotheses**
2.	The statement that specifies a hypothesized value for one or more of the population parameters is the _____.	**null hypothesis**
3.	The null hypotheses is symbolized as _____.	H_o
4.	The statement that asserts that the population parameter is some value other than that hypothesized is the _____.	**alternative hypothesis**
5.	The alternative hypothesis is symbolized as _____.	H_1
6.	In the study of coin tosses, the null hypothesis is that the coin is _____.	**unbiased**
7.	In the study of coin tosses, the alternative hypothesis is that the coin is _____.	**biased**
8.	The alternative hypothesis may either_____ or _____.	**directional, non-directional**
9.	A non-directional alternative hypothesis may also be called a _____.	**two-tailed hypothesis**
10.	A directional alternative hypothesis may also be called a _____.	**one-tailed hypothesis**
11.	The null hypothesis can never be _____.	**proved**
12.	Although the null hypothesis can never be proved, we can assert that there is no basis for its _____.	**rejection**
13.	To reject the null hypothesis is to state that the _____ is of some value other than the one hypothesized.	**population parameter**

14. The support of the alternative hypothesis is always _____. **indirect**

15. We can never prove the null hypothesis by rejecting the _____. **alternative hypothesis**

Objective 6. *Explain the two types of error that must be considered in the testing of statistical hypotheses.*

1. The rejection of a null hypothesis that is actually true is a _____. **type I error**

2. The probability of making a type I error is _____. **alpha**

3. At the .05 level of significance , we will commit a _____ 5% of the time. **type I error**

4. The failure to reject a null hypothesis that is actually false is a _____. **type II error**

5. The probability of committing a type II error is _____. **beta**

6. The lower we set the rejection level, the lower the probability of a _____. **type I error**

7. The lower we set the rejection level, the greater the probability of a _____. **type II error**

8. Type I and type II errors are both cases of _____ errors. **sampling**

9. There is no need for statistical inference if the _____ are known. **population parameters**

10. Using the .05 significance level, approximately 1 out of every 20 students who rejects the null hypothesis is making a _____. **type I error**

Objective 7. *Explain some of the precautions that are necessary in the interpretation of statistical tests.*

1. All scientific knowledge is _____ rather than absolute. **probabilistic**

2. Statistical significance must be interpreted within a _____. **meaningful context**

3.   If a hypothesis is tested at the .05 significance level and the   **null**
      probability of the result occurring by chance is .06, we cannot   **hypothesis**
      reject the _____.

4.   Large samples are more likely to result in_____ findings   **statistically**
      than are small samples.   **significant**

Multiple Choice Questions

1.   A complete or theoretical set of individuals, objects, or   **b**
      measurements having some common observable characteristics
      is a _____.

      a.   variable   c.   sample
      b.   population   d.   parameter

2.   The mathematical characteristics of populations are called: **c**

      a.   statistics   c.   parameters
      b.   indicators   d.   constants

3.   Population parameters are inferred from: **c**

      a.   random number tables
      b.   nonparametric statistics
      c.   sample statistics
      d.   intervening variables

4.   The probability distribution of the possible values of a statistic is a: **a**

      a.   sampling distribution   c.   leptokurtic distribution
      b.   normal distribution   d.   symmetrical distribution

5.   A sampling distribution is _____ probability distribution.   **c**

      a.   an empirical   c.   a theoretical
      b.   a classical   d.   a binomial

6.   The possible values of the sample statistics in a sampling distribution   **a**
      result from drawing all possible samples of a:

      a.   fixed size from the same population
      b.   fixed size from different populations
      c.   variable size from the same populations
      d.   variable size from different populations

7. Compared to the actual distribution of scores in the population, the sampling distribution of means will have a: **c**

   a. smaller mean
   b. larger mean
   c. smaller standard deviation
   d. larger standard deviation

8. The sampling distribution is one of the most important concepts in _____ statistics.   **b**

   a. intuitive   c. deductive
   b. inferential   d. descriptive

9. As a direct result of a sampling distribution, it is possible to: **d**

   a. predict independent variables
   b. predict dependent variables
   c. compute correlations
   d. test hypotheses

10. The two basic models of a sampling distribution are the: **b**

   a. skewed distribution and leptokurtic distribution
   b. normal distribution and binomial distribution
   c. skewed distribution and normal distribution
   d. leptokurtic distribution and binomial distribution

11. The true proportion of heads and tails characterizing a coin: **d**

   a. is $P = \frac{1}{2}$
   b. is $Q = \frac{1}{2}$
   c. can be determined by sample tosses
   d. can never be known

12. Although, the true value of heads and tails is unknowable, the value can be estimated by: **c**

   a. partial correlation   c. simple random sampling
   b. multiple regression   d. magnitude estimation

13. In the coin problem, the probability of the occurrence of heads is symbolized as _____.   **a**

   a. P c. T
   b. Q d. Z

14. The normal distribution is a model for a sampling distribution with _____ variables. **a**

a. continuous
b. dichotomous
c. nominal-level
d. ordinal-level

15. The binomial distribution is a model for a sampling distribution with _____ variables. **b**

a. continuous
b. dichotomous
c. interval-level
d. ratio-level

16. The statistical cutoff point is the basis for asserting that a particular finding has resulted from the operation of: **d**

a. the independent variable
b. the interviewing variable
c. chance factors
d. nonchance factors

17. The statistical cutoff point for inferring the operation of nonchance factors is called the: **c**

a. extremely limit
b. difference magnitude
c. significance level
d. probability estimate

18. The two significance levels most frequently used as statistical cutoff points are: **c**

a. .5 and .1
b. .1 and .05
c. .05 and .01
d. .01 and .001

19. The level of significance is also called the _____ level. **a**

a. alpha
b. beta
c. delta
d. theta

20. According to the text, the alpha level should be: **a**

a. established before the research is conducted
b. established after the findings are analyzed
c. set to make all findings significant
d. set to make all finds nonsignificant

21.   A statement that specifies hypothesized values for one or   c
       more of the population parameters is the:

       a.   probability theorem
       b.   standard error of estimate
       c.   null hypothesis
       d.   alternative hypothesis

22.   The statement that asserts that the population parameter is of some   d
       value other than the one hypothesized is the:

       a.   probability theorem
       b.   standard error of estimate
       c.   null hypothesis
       d.   alternative hypothesis

23.   The alternative hypothesis is symbolized as: c

       a. H c. H_1
       b. H_0 d. H_2

24.   The null hypothesis is symbolized as: b

       a. H c. H_1
       b. H_0 d. H_2

25.   According to the text, an alternative hypothesis may be either: b

       a.   normal or nonnormal
       b.   directional or nondirectional
       c.   parametric or nonparametric
       d.   linear or nonlinear

26.   A directional alternative hypothesis requires the   b
       use of _____ probability values.

       a.   one-tailed   c.   discrete
       b.   two-tailed   d.   continuous

27.   According to the logic of statistical inference, which of the   c
       following statements is permissible?

       a.   the null hypothesis is false
       b.   the alternative hypothesis is false
       c.   there is no basis for rejecting the null hypothesis
       d.   there is no basis for rejecting the alternative hypothesis

28. According to the logic of statistical inference, the support   **b**
    of the alternative hypothesis is always:

    a.   direct   c.   reciprocal
    b.   indirect   d.   circular

29. The logic of statistical inference proceeds on the assumption that: **a**

    a.   the null hypothesis is true
    b.   the null hypothesis is false
    c.   the null hypothesis is neither true nor false
    d.   the alternative hypothesis is true

30. The logic of statistical inference requires that scientific   **c**
    findings be regarded as:

    a.   absolute statements   c.   probability statements
    b.   relative statements   d.   contextual statements

31. The rejection of a null hypothesis when it is actually true is a: **c**

    a.   standard error   c.   type I error
    b.   scaling error   d.   type II error

32. The failure to reject a null hypothesis that is actually false is a: **d**

    a.   standard error   c.   type I error
    b.   scaling error   d.   type II error

33. The probability of committing a type II error is: **b**

    a.   alpha   c.   delta
    b.   beta   d.   theta

34. According to the text: **d**

    a.   type I errors are more avoidable than type II errors
    b.   type II errors are more serious than type I errors
    c.   type I errors are more numerous than type II errors
    d.   type II errors are more numerous than type I errors

35. The probabilities of a type I error and a type II error are: **b**

    a.   directly related   c.   unrelated
    b.   inversely related   d.   identical

36.   When population parameters are known: **d**

     a.   type I errors become more serious than type II errors
     b.   type II errors become more serious than type I errors
     c.   statistical inference becomes more complicated
     d.   statistical inference becomes unnecessary

37.   Compared to smaller samples, larger samples are more likely to   **a**
     yield:

     a.   statistically significant findings
     b.   statistically nonsignificant findings
     c.   scaling errors
     d.   type II error

38.   The alternative hypothesis always states: **d**

     a.   a specific value
     b.   a value that can prove the null hypothesis
     c.   a value that can lead to a type II error
     d.   a value that can be accepted as a result of the rejection of
         the null hypothesis

39.   Which of the following cannot be a null hypothesis?   **d**

     a.   The population means are equal
     b. $P = Q = 1/2$
     c. $P = 1/4, Q = 3/4$
     d.   The sample means are equal

40.   The rejection of H_o is always: **c**

     a.   Direct
     b.   Based on rejection of H_1
     c.   Based on the direct proof of H_1
     d.   Indirect

41.   If the H_1 is directional, we must calculate   **a**

     a.   A one-tailed p-value
     b.   A two-tailed p-value
     c.   A confidence interval
     d.   The degrees of freedom

Chapter 14

STATISTICAL INFERENCE AND CONTINUOUS VARIABLES

Learning Objectives

After mastering the content of this chapter, you should be able to:

1. *Explain the characteristics of the sampling distribution of the mean.*

2. *Explain the procedures for testing statistical hypotheses when the population parameters are known.*

3. *Explain Student's t as a test of statistical hypotheses with unknown population parameters.*

4. *Explain interval estimation as a technique for inferring population parameters.*

5. *Explain the use of confidence intervals and confidence limits in the estimation of population parameters.*

6. *Explain the sampling distribution and the test of significance for Pearson's r.*

7. *Explain the sampling distribution and the test of significance for Goodman and Kruskal's gamma.*

Programmed Review

Objective 1. *Explain the characteristics of the sampling distribution of the mean.*

1.	The procedure that permits estimation of population parameters from sample statistics is called _____.	**statistical inference**
2.	The mean of the sampling distribution of means is *not* affected by _____.	**sample size**
3.	However, sample size does effect the _____ of the sampling distribution of means.	**standard deviation**
4.	In a sampling distribution, the standard deviation of the sampling means is called the _____	**standard error of the mean**
5.	The mean of the sampling distribution will vary with a change in _____.	**sample size**
6.	The sampling error of the mean is interpreted in the same way that the standard deviation is interpreted with respect to the _____.	**N**
7.	If each of the means in a sampling distribution is treated as a raw score, the standard deviation computed for this distribution is called the _____.	**standard error of the mean**
8.	The standard error of the mean is interpreted in the same way that the standard deviation is interpreted with respect to the _____.	**normal curve**
9.	The distribution of sample means drawn from a normally distributed population will be _____.	**normal**
10.	The mean of the sample means is equal to the _____.	**population mean**
11.	It is known that the distribution of sample means of a nonnormal population will approach the form of a _____ as the sample size increases.	**normal curve**
12.	The relationship described in the previous statement is dictated by the _____.	**central limit theorem**

Objective 2. *Explain the procedures for testing statistical hypotheses when the population parameters are known.*

1.	Estimates of population parameters that involve the use of single sample values are called _____.	**point estimates**
2.	In making inferences about population parameters, we compare our sample results with the expected results given by a _____.	**sampling distribution**
3.	A sample variance that uses N in the denominator provides a _____ of the population variance.	**biased estimate**
4.	A sample variance that uses $N - 1$ in its denominator provides an _____ of the population variance.	**unbiased estimate**
5.	The biased estimate of the population variance is appropriate if we are describing the variability of a _____.	**sample**
6.	On the average, an unbiased estimate will equal the value of _____.	$\dfrac{\Sigma \,(X - \bar{X})^2}{N - 1}$
7.	The unbiased estimate of the population variance is symbolized as _____.	$\hat{S}^2$

Objective 3. *Explain Student's t as a test of statistical hypotheses with unknown population parameters.*

1.	The statistic that is tested with the t distribution is called _____.	**Student's t**
2.	Student's t is expressed in the mathematical form of a _____.	**ratio**
3.	For the t statistic, the family of distributions varies as a function of _____.	**degrees of freedom (df)**
4.	The degrees of freedom refer to the number of values that are free to vary after we have placed certain _____.	**restrictions**
5.	When there is a single restriction on a sample, the number of degrees of freedom is _____.	$N - 1$
6.	The use of Student's t depends on the assumption that the underlying population is _____.	**normally distributed**
7.	A test that yields valid statistical inferences when there are large departures from normality in the population distribution is said to be _____.	**robust**

8. If there are serious doubts about the normality of the population distribution, it is useful to increase the _____ in each sample.   **N**

9. The family of *t* distributions is distributed symmetrically about a mean of _____.   **zero**

10. Compared to the normal curve, the dispersion of the *t* distributions is _____.   **larger**

11. The *t* distributions resemble the normal curve as_____ increases.   **sample size**

Objective 4. *Explain interval estimation as a technique for inferring population parameters.*

1. The two subproblems that arise in the estimation of parameters from statistics are _____ estimation and _____ estimation.   **point, interval**

2. Point estimation is the estimation of parameters from _____ sample values.   **single**

3. Interval estimation is a technique for including or encompassing the population parameter within a _____.   **range of values**

4. Our confidence in a particular interval estimation may be expressed in terms of _____.   **probabilities**

Objective 5. *Explain the use of confidence intervals and confidence limits in the estimation of population parameters.*

1. The range of values that results from an interval estimation is called a _____.   **confidence interval**

2. A confidence interval for the population mean specifies a range of values bounded by two _____.   **endpoints**

3. The two endpoints of a confidence interval are called the _____.   **confidence limits**

4. One may conclude that a confidence interval will include the population mean a certain _____ of the time.   **percent**

5. In addition to raw scores, confidence intervals and limits can also be computed for _____ and _____.   **percentages, proportions**

6. In the computation of a confidence interval for proportions, we must first determine the _____.   **standard error of the proportion**

Objective 6. *Explain the sampling distribution and the test of significance for Pearson's r.*

1. The values of Pearson's *r* may range from _____ to _____.   **-1, +1**

2. In statistical inference, the null hypothesis most frequently investigated with one-sample case of correlation is that the population correlation coefficient is _____.   **zero**

3. The symbol for the population correlation coefficient is _____. ρ

4. The sampling distribution of ρ is usually _____.   **nonnormal**

5. When testing the null hypothesis that the population correlation is zero, the appropriate statistic is _____.   **Student's *t***

6. In the equation for testing the null hypothesis that the population correlation is zero, the sample correlation is symbolized as _____.   *r*

7. When testing the null hypothesis that the population correlation is zero, the number of pairs is symbolized as _____.   *N*

8. The *t* should *not* be used for testing hypotheses other than the population correlation being equal to _____.   **zero**

9. When the null hypothesis states a population correlation that is different from zero, the appropriate sampling distribution is the _____.   **normal distribution**

10. The test statistic for Fisher's transformation is _____.   *z*

11. In Fisher's transformation, the transformed value of the correlation is symbolized as _____. z_r

12. In Fisher's transformation, the transformed valued of the population correlation specified by H_o is symbolized as _____. z_r

Objective 7. *Explain the sampling distribution and the test of significance for Goodman and Kruskal's gamma.*

1. Gamma is a measure of association for _____ data. **ordinal level**

2. The appropriate sampling distribution for testing the significance of gamma is the _____. **normal distribution**

3. The appropriate test statistic for gamma is _____. **z**

4. In the equation for testing the significance of gamma, the value of gamma is symbolized as _____. **G**

5. In the equation for testing the significance of gamma, the number of concordant pairs is symbolized as _____. **C**

6. In the equation for testing the significance of gamma, the number of discordant pairs is symbolized as _____. **D**

7. In the equation for testing the significance of gamma, the population value assumed by the null hypothesis is symbolized as _____. **γ**

Multiple Choice Questions

1. The purpose of statistical inference is to estimate: **c**

   a. sample statistics   c. population parameters
   b. expected frequencies   d. levels of measurement

2. The sampling distribution for a discrete two-category nominal variable is the: **b**

   a. normal distribution   c. *t* distribution
   b. binomial distribution d. *F* distribution

3. The standard deviation of the sampling distribution of means is called the: **b**

   a. *z* score   c. *t* distribution
   b. standard error of the mean d. confidence interval

158

4. The probability of selecting a _____ with an extreme   **c**
    mean is less than the probability of selecting a single score
    that is equally extreme.

    a. population   c. sample
    b. variable   d. confidence interval

5. The probability of drawing extreme values of a sample mean   **c**
    decline as:

    a. p increases   c. N increases
    b. p decreases   d. N decreases

6. If each of the sample means of a sampling distribution is   **c**
    treated as a raw score, the standard deviation of this
    distribution is referred to as the:

    a. mean square
    b. sum of squares
    c. standard error of the mean
    d. standard error of the proportion

7. The standard error of the mean is interpreted with respect to the: **a**

    a. normal distribution   c. binomial distribution
    b. t distribution   d. F distribution

8. The distribution of sample means drawn from a normally   **a**
    distributed population is:

    a. normal   c. platykurtic
    b. leptokurtic   d. rectangular

9. The mean of a sampling distribution of means is equal to: **c**

    a. the sum of squares   c. the population mean
    b. the population variance   d. the confidence interval

10. Increasing the sample size of a sampling distribution of means will: **d**

    a. increase the mean
    b. decrease the mean
    c. increase the standard error of the mean
    d. decrease the standard error of the mean

11.   The finding that a sampling distribution of means drawn from   **a**
       any population approaches normality is stated by the:

       a.   central limit theorem
       b.   confidence interval
       c.   biased estimate of the population variance
       d.   *t* distribution

12.   The central limit theorem states that the distribution of sample   **c**
       means approaches normality as:

       a.   the mean becomes larger
       b.   the mean becomes smaller
       c.   *N* becomes larger
       d.   *N* becomes smaller

13.   According to the central limit theorem, the distribution of   **b**
       sample means from a skewed population approaches the form
       of the _____ as *N* increases.

       a.   binomial distribution   c.   *t* distribution
       b.   normal distribution   d.   leptokurtic distribution

14.   The portion of area under the normal curve that includes   **c**
       those values of a statistic that lead to rejection of the null
       hypothesis is:

       a.   an endpoint   c.   a critical region
       b.   an end zone   d.   an improbable region

15.   The critical region for a statistical test is determined by the: **b**

       a.   standard error of the mean
       b.   level of significance
       c.   law of large numbers
       d.   *t* distribution

16.   The estimates of population parameters from single sample   **b**
       values are called:

       a.   interval estimates   c.   confidence estimates
       b.   point estimates   d.   regression estimates

17. The sum of the squared deviations of each score from the mean divided by N is called the:

    a. biased estimate of the sample variance
    b. unbiased estimate of the sample variance
    c. biased estimate of the population variance
    d. unbiased estimate of the population variance

    c

18. The sum of the squared deviations of each score from the mean divided by $N - 1$ is called the:

    a. biased estimate of the sample variance
    b. unbiased estimate of the sample variance
    c. biased estimate of the population variance
    d. unbiased estimate of the population variance

    d

19. On the average, an unbiased estimate will be

    a. equal to the value of the statistic
    b. larger than the mean
    c. equal to the value of the parameter
    d. larger than the parameter

    c

20. The family of t distributions is determined by the:

    a. standard errors of the mean
    b. point estimates
    c. degrees of freedom
    d. law of large numbers

    c

21. With very large degrees of freedom, the t distribution begins to approximate a:

    a. binomial distribution   c. skewed distribution
    b. leptokurtic distribution   d. normal distribution

    d

22. If the means and variances of two samples differ in any systematic way, then the underlying population:

    a. must be normal   c. must be skewed
    b. cannot be normal   d. cannot be skewed

    b

23. A statistical test that leads to valid inference despite large departures from normality in the population is said to be:

    a. rigorous   c. systematic
    b. robust   d. unbiased

    b

24.   The robustness of Student's *t* ratio is a direct result of the: **b**

   a.   law of large numbers
   b.   central limit theorem
   c.   law of diminishing returns
   d.   additive rule of probability

25.   If there are serious doubts about the normality of a population   **b**
       distribution, the best procedure is to:

   a.   increase the number of samples
   b.   increase the *N* in each sample
   c.   increase the critical region
   d.   decrease the critical region

26.   The proportion of area under a curve that includes the values   **b**
       of any statistic that rejects the null hypothesis is the:

   a.   confidence interval   c.   standard deviation
   b.   critical region   d.   standard error of the mean

27.   The critical values that bound the critical regions correspond to: **c**

   a.   standard errors   c.   levels of significance
   b.   population parameters   d.   degrees of freedom

28.   Compared to the normal distribution, *t* distributions have: **c**

   a.   higher means   c.   greater dispersion
   b.   lower means   d.   lesser dispersion

29.   The technique for estimating a range of values that is likely to   **d**
       include the population parameter is:

   a.   range estimation   c.   area estimation
   b.   point estimation   d.   interval estimation

30.   The direct outcome of interval estimation is called a: **a**

   a.   confidence interval   c.   standard interval
   b.   normal interval   d.   distribution

31.   The two endpoints of a confidence interval define the: **c**

   a.   confidence parameters   c.   confidence limits
   b.   confidence range   d.   confidence sets

32. The probabilities of the two most frequently used confidence intervals are: **d**

   a.   1% and 5%   c.   5% and 95%
   b.   1% and 95%   d.   95% and 99%

33. The finding that the standard error of the mean decreases as sample size increases follows directly from the: **b**

   a.   central limit theorem
   b.   law of large numbers
   c.   law of diminishing returns
   d.   additive rule of probability

34. When the sample size is less than 50, the appropriate distribution for computing confidence intervals for a population mean is the: **a**

   a. t distribution   c.   normal distribution
   b. z distribution   d. F distribution

35. In computing confidence intervals for percentages and proportions, the appropriate sampling distribution for r is the: **c**

   a. F distribution   c. z distribution
   b. t distribution   d.   leptokurtic distribution

36. Given the null hypothesis that the population correlation is zero, the most appropriate sampling distribution for r is the: **c**

   a.   binomial distribution   c. t distribution
   b. z distribution   d. F distribution

37. The appropriate sampling distribution for testing the significance for gamma is the: **b**

   a.   binomial distribution   c. t distribution
   b. z distribution   d. F distribution

38. In a normally distributed population with $\mu = 20$, $\sigma = 5$, which of the following sizes will yield the smallest variation among sample means? N equals: **d**

   a.   1   c.   20
   b.   5   d.   250

163

39. In a normally distributed population with $\mu = 15$, $\sigma = 4$,   **d**
     we draw, with replacement, samples of $N = 2$. Which pair of
     scores is least likely to be selected:

     a.   12, 18   c.   16, 14
     b.   15, 15   d.   11, 19

40. In a normally distributed population with $\mu = 50$, $\sigma = 10$, we   **c**
     draw samples of $N = 9$. The standard error of the mean is:

     a.   .90   c.   3.33
     b.   1.11   d.   3.57

41. In a normally distributed population with an unknown mean,   **a**
     which of the following samples sizes is likely to most
     closely approximate μ? N equals:

     a.   250   c.   20
     b.   5   d.   50

42. Given: $\sigma = 20$, $\mu = 210$, $N = 16$, the appropriate statistic for   **c**
     testing H_0: $\mu = 200$ yields a value of:

     a.   1.93   c.   2.00
     b.   8.20   d.   2.24

43. Given: $\alpha = .05$, $\bar{X} = 16$, $s = 4$, $N = 30$, the number of degrees of   **d**
     freedom is:

     a.   17   c.   15
     b.   3   d.   29

Thought Problems

Assume the following distribution of scores: 1, 2, 3, 4.

1.   Compute the biased estimate of the population variance.

2.   Compute the unbiased estimate of the population variance.

3.   Compute the biased estimate of the population standard deviation.

4.   Compute the unbiased estimate of the population standard deviation.

5.   State the appropriate sampling distribution for testing the null hypothesis that a
     population correlation is zero.

6. State the appropriate sampling distribution for testing the null hypothesis that a population correlation is other than zero.

7. State the appropriate sampling distribution for testing the significance of gamma.

Essay Questions

1. If samples are randomly drawn from the *same* population, would we expect the obtained means to differ from sample to sample?

2. What happens to the variability of the sample means as we increase the sample size?

3. What is the relationship between level of significance and confidence interval?

4. Why is it usually inappropriate to use *z* as a test statistic?

5. Is the sample mean an unbiased estimate of the population mean?

6. Is there more than one *t*-distribution? On what do they depend?

Answers

Thought Problems

1.	1.25	5.	*t* distribution
2.	1.67	6.	*z* distribution
3.	1.12	7.	*z* distribution
4.	1.29		

Essay Questions

1.   Yes. This is due to the operation of uncontrolled chance factors.

2.   The variability decreases.

3.   The critical values at a given level of significance bracket the confidence interval. Thus, the critical upper and lower values at $\alpha = .05$, two-tailed test, include 95% of the area-- the region of acceptance of H_o.

4.   It is rare that we know the population variance and standard deviation. For very large samples, *z* may be substituted for *t* but little is gained in the way of computational ease.

5.   Yes, as long as the sample is drawn from the population by some random process.

6.   Yes. There is a separate *t*-distribution for each number of degrees of freedom. This is why *t*-distributions are rarely published but critical values are.

Chapter 15

AN INTRODUCTION TO THE ANALYSIS OF VARIANCE

Learning Objectives

After mastering the content of this chapter, you should be able to:

1. *Explain the logic of testing multigroup comparisons with a single statistic.*

2. *Explain the concept and the computation of sums of squares.*

3. *Explain the two independent variance estimates in the analysis of variance.*

4. *Explain the fundamental concepts of analysis of variance.*

5. *Explain the assumptions underlying the use of analysis of variance.*

6. *Describe the steps in the computation of an analysis of variance for three groups.*

7. *Explain the interpretation of the F statistic and the uses of comparisons between pairs of means.*

Programmed Review

Objective 1. *Explain the logic of testing multigroup comparisons with a single statistic.*

1.	Many research designs require a comparison of more than _____.	**two groups**
2.	The use of the *t*-ratio for multiple comparisons among three or more groups increases the probability of a _____.	**type I error**
3.	The statistical technique that permits a single comparison among three or more independent samples is the_____.	**analysis of variance**
4.	When the analysis of variance is used for two independent samples, its probability values are identical to the _____.	**t-ratio**
5.	When the analysis of variance is used for three of more levels of a single independent variable it is called a _____ analysis of variance.	**one-way**
6.	The analysis of variance is abbreviated as _____.	**ANOVA**

Objective 2. *Explain the concept and the computation of sums of squares.*

1.	In the case of several samples, the sum of the squared deviations from the grand mean is the _____.	**total sum of squares**
2.	The total sum of squares is a measure of the total _____ in the data.	**variation**
3.	The total sum of squares is symbolized as _____.	SS_{tot}
4.	The sum of squares obtained within each sample is called the_____.	**within-group sum of squares**
5.	The within-group sum of squares is symbolized as _____.	SS_w
6.	The sum of the squared deviations of each group mean from the grand mean is the _____.	**between-group sum of squares**
7.	The between-group sum of squares is symbolized as _____.	SS_{bet}
8.	The total sum of squares is equal to _____.	$SS_w + SS_{bet}$

9. The term that describes the effects of the independent variable is _____. **SS_bet**

$$SS_{bet}$$

Objective 3. *Explain the two independent variable estimates in the analysis of variance.*

1. The analysis of variance requires that we obtain _____ estimates of variance. **two independent**

2. In the analysis of variance, the ratio of the between-group variance to the within-group variance is the _____. **test statistic**

3. The statistic for the analysis variance is tested on the _____. ***F*-distribution**

4. In the computation of the *F*-ratio, the between and within-group variances are divided by their respective _____. **degrees of freedom**

5. The degrees of freedom of the between-group sum of squares is symbolized as _____. ***k* - 1**

6. The degrees of freedom of the within-group sum of squares is symbolized as _____. ***N* - *k***

7. Since any difference among the sample means will enlarge the value of *F*, the analysis of variance is a _____ test. **two-tailed**

Objective 4. *Explain the fundamental concepts of analysis of variance.*

1. For two or more groups it is possible to identify two different bases for estimating the population variance: the _____ and the _____. **between-group, within-group**

2. The between-group variance estimate reflects the extent of the difference among the _____. **group means**

3. The within-group variance estimate reflects the variation of the scores within each _____. **treatment group**

4. The statement that two or more samples have been drawn from populations with the same sample mean is the _____. **null hypothesis**

5. The statement that the samples are not drawn from a population of the same mean is the _____. **alternative hypothesis**

6. The between-group variance estimate divided by the within-group variance estimate is the _____. ***F*-ratio**

169

7. In the two-sample case, the *F*-ratio yields probability values that are identical to the _____. **_t_-ratio**

8. For the two-sample case, the value of *F* is_____. **t^2**

Objective 5. *Explain the assumptions underlying the use of analysis of variance.*

1. A basic assumption underlying the analysis of variance is that the within-group variances are _____. **homogenous**

2. In addition to the assumption of homogenous variance, the analysis of variance requires the assumption of _____ within groups, random and _____ sampling, _____ scaling for the dependent variable, and _____ scaling for the independent variables. **normality, independent, interval, nominal**

Objective 6. *Describe the steps in the computation of an analysis of variance for three groups.*

1. The division of the between-group sum of squares by *k* - 1 degrees of freedom provides the between group _____. **mean square**

2. The division of the between-groups sum of squares by *k* - 1 degrees of freedom provides the within group _____. **mean square**

3. The ratio of the between-group variance estimate to the within-group variance estimate is the _____. **_F_-ratio**

Objective 7. *Explain the interpretation of the F statistic and the uses of comparisons between pairs of means.*

1. The finding of an overall significant *F*-ratio permits investigation intended to determine exactly which pairs of means are _____. **significantly different**

2. In the absence of a significant *F*-ratio, any significant differences between specific pairs of mean must be regarded as _____. **chance differences**

3 Comparisons between pairs of means that are planned in advance of the investigation are _____comparisons. **_a priori_**

4. Comparisons between pairs of means that are *not* planned in advance of the investigation are _____ comparisons. **_a posteriori_**

5. Tukey's test for pairwise comparisons among means is called the _____ test. **HSD**

6. The HSD attempts to identify _____ between means.

Multiple Choice Questions

1. In the two-sample case, the probability values yielded by the analysis of variance are identical to the:

   d

   a. binomial distribution
   b. trinomial distribution
   c. normal distribution
   d. t-ratio

2. In a study with three or more samples, the use of t-ratios for multiple paired comparisons:

   c

   a. violates the assumption of homogeneity of variance.
   b. decreases the probability of a type I error.
   c. increases the probability of a type I error.
   d. violates the assumption of normality

3. The one-way analysis of variance derives its name from the fact that the samples represent different categories or levels of a single:

   b

   a. dependent variable
   b. independent variable
   c. criterion variable
   d. control variable

4. In experimental research, the independent variable is called the:

   d

   a. criterion variable
   b. control variable
   c. matched variable
   d. treatment variable

5. In the analysis of variance, the sum of the squared deviations of each score from the grand mean is the:

   a

   a. SS_{tot}
   b. SS_{w}
   c. SS_{bet}
   d. SS_{est}

6. In the computation of analysis variance, the sum of the squared deviations of each score from its sample mean is the:

   b

   a. SS_{tot}
   b. SS_{w}
   c. SS_{bet}
   d. SS_{est}

7. In the computation of analysis of variance, the sum of the squared deviations of each sample mean from the grand mean multiplied by N in each group is the:

    a. SS_{tot} c. SS_{bet}
    b. SS_{w} d. SS_{est}

c

8. The measure of the variation that is directly attributable to the independent variable is the:

    a.   total sum of squares   c.   within sum of squares
    b.   between sum of squares   d.   residual sum of squares

b

9. The within sum of squares is a measure of the variation in the dependent variable that *cannot* be attributed to:

    a.   measurement error   c.   individual differences
    b.   random error   d.   the independent variable

d

10. The estimates of variance are the sums of squares:

    a.   added to the degrees of freedom
    b.   subtracted from the degrees of freedom
    c.   multiplied by the degrees of freedom
    d.   divided by the degrees of freedom

d

11. The degrees of freedom of the between-group sum of squares is:

    a. $N - 1$ c. $N - k$
    b. $k - 1$ d. $N - 2$

b

12. The degrees of freedom of the within-groups sum of squares is:

    a. $N - 1$ c. $N - k$
    b. $k - 1$ d. $N - 2$

c

13. In the analysis of variance, the ratio of the two mean squares is the:

    a.   significance level   c.   test statistic
    b. F distribution   d. t-ratio

c

14. The test statistic for the analysis of variance is the:

    a. t-ratio   c. z score
    b. F-ratio   d.   percentile

b

15. In the analysis of variance, the difference among the group   **b**
means are estimated by the:

   a.   total variance   c.   within-group variance
   b.   between-group variance   d.   regression variance

16. In the analysis of variance, the dispersion of scores within   **c**
each sample is the estimate of:

   a.   total variance   c.   within-group variance
   b.   between-group variance   d.   regression variance

17. The estimate that is often referred to as the error term is the: **c**

   a.   total variance   c.   within-group variance
   b.   between-group variance   d.   regression variance

18. For the two-sample case, the value of the F-ratio is equal to: **b**

   a. t c. z
   b. t^2 d. z^2

19. Which of the following is not one of the assumptions of   **c**
the analysis of variance:

   a.   random and independent sampling
   b.   interval scaling for the dependent variable
   c.   interval scaling for the independent variable
   d.   normality within samples

20. In the calculation of analysis of variance, the first step   **b**
is computation of the:

   a.   between-group sum of squares
   b.   total sum of squares
   c.   within-group sum of squares
   d.   within-group variance estimate

21. In the analysis of variance, the F-statistic is the ratio: **c**

   a.   total variance to the between-group variance
   b.   between-group variance to the total variance
   c.   between-group variance to the within-group variance
   d.   within-group variance to the between-group variance

22. Given a study with four samples and nine scores within each sample, the appropriate degrees of freedom for testing the F ratio are:

    a. 3 and 32   c. 3 and 36
    b. 4 and 32   d. 4 and 36

    a

23. In the event of a significant F-ratio, a planned comparison between any pair of sample means is _____ comparison.

    a. a *post hoc*   c. an *a priori*
    b. an *ad hoc*   d. an *a posteriori*

    c

24. In the event of a significant F-ratio, an unplanned comparison between pairs of sample means is_____ comparison.

    a. a *post hoc*   c. an *a priori*
    b. an *ad hoc*   d. an *a posteriori*

    d

25. Tukey's measure for paired comparisons among sample means is the_____ test.

    a. PRE   c. FAIR
    b. HSD   d. ANOVA

    b

26. If you obtained an F-ratio equal to .69 with df = 2/220 you would conclude that:

    a. there were no significant differences in means
    b. you had made an error
    c. the variances were equal
    d. the null hypothesis was rejected

    a

27. If the mean for each of the treatment groups were identical, the F-ratio would be:

    a. 1.00
    b. zero
    c. a positive number between 0 and 1.00
    d. a negative number

    b

28. To obtain the between-groups variance estimate, you divide the between-groups sum of squares by:

    a. $N - 1$ degrees of freedom
    b. N degrees of freedom
    c. $k - 1$ degrees of freedom
    d. within-groups sum squares

    c

29. In the analysis of variance in the two-sample case: **d**

    a. $F = t^2$
    b. it is possible to identify two different bases for estimating the population variance
    c. $df_w = N - k$
    d. all of the above

30. The between-group variance estimate: **b**

    a. is associated with $df = N - k$
    b. reflects the magnitude of the difference among the group means
    c. is referred to as the error term
    d. all of the above

31. The independent variables in analysis of variance **b**

    a. must be correlated
    b. may be measured nominal scales
    c. must be at least interval scales
    d. should be ratio scales

32. If we were to perform multiple t-tests---without benefit of an analysis of variance---with a several-group experiment, we would be running an increased risk of: **c**

    a. violating the design
    b. extending the *t*-distributions beyond their *df* limitation
    c. a Type I error
    d. none of the above

Thought Problems

Assume the following independent samples of scores:

X_1	X_2	X_3
1	4	7
2	5	8
3	6	9

1. Compute the total sum of squares.

2. Compute the between-group sum of squares.

3. Compute the within-group sum of squares.

4. State the degrees of freedom for the total sum of squares.

5. State the degrees of freedom for the between-group sum of squares.

6. State the degrees of freedom for the within-group sum squares.

7. State the value of the F-ratio.

Assume the following independent samples of scores:

X_1	X_2	X_3
1	2	3
4	5	6
7	8	9

8. Compute the total sum of squares.

9. Compute the between-group of squares.

10. Compute the within-group sum of squares.

11. State the degrees of freedom for the total sum of squares.

12. State the degrees of freedom for the between-group sum squares.

13. State the degrees of freedom for the within-group sum of squares.

14. State the value of the F-ratio.

Assume the following independent samples of scores.

X_1	X_2	X_3	X_4
1	2	3	4
5	6	7	8

15. Compute the total sum of squares.

16. Compute the between-group sum of squares.

17.   Compute the within-group sum of squares.

18.   State the degrees of freedom for the total sum of squares.

19.   State the degrees of freedom for the between-group sum of squares.

20.   State the degrees of freedom for the within-group sum of squares.

21.   State the value of the F-ratio.

Computational Problems

A sociologist compares the annual family incomes of Protestants, Catholics, and Jews. He obtain the following scores:

Protestants	Catholics	Jews
14k	15k	17k
16k	16k	18k
13k	8k	11k
18k	9k	9k
19k	11k	20k
20k	13k	13k
11k		17k
14k		

1.   Compute the total sum of squares.

2.   Compute the between-group of squares.

3.   Compute the within-group of squares.

4.   State the degrees of freedom for the total sum of squares.

5.   State the degrees of freedom for the between-group sum of squares.

6.   State the degrees of freedom for the within-group sum of squares.

7.   State the value of the F-ratio.

Answers

Thought Problems

1.	60	8.	60	15.	42
2.	54	9.	6	16.	10
3.	6	10.	54	17.	32
4.	8	11.	8	18.	7
5.	2	12.	2	19.	3
6.	6	13.	6	20.	4
7.	27	14.	.33	21.	.42

Computational Problems

1.	268.95	5.	2
2.	49.08	6.	18
3.	219.87	7.	2.01
4.	20		

Chapter 16

STATISTICAL INFERENCE WITH CATEGORICAL VARIABLES: CHI SQUARE AND RELATED MEASURES

Learning Objectives

After mastering the content of this chapter, you should be able to:

1. *Explain why nonparametric statistical tests are needed for certain kinds of research problems.*

2. *Explain the use and computation of χ^2 for the one-variable case.*

3. *Explain the limitations in the use of χ^2.*

4. *Explain the use and computation of three nominal measures of association based on χ^2.*

Programmed Review

Objective 1. *Explain why nonparametric statistical tests are needed for certain kinds of research problems.*

1.	Many of the new variables in social science research do not lead themselves to traditional_____ statistical research.	**parametric**
2.	Parametric statistical tests are inappropriate for variables measured at the_____ and _____ levels.	**nominal, ordinal**
3.	Nonparametric tests do not require any assumptions about the shape of the _____.	**population distribution**
4.	With small sample sizes and badly skewed distributions, a nonparametric test may be as _____ as its parametric counterpart.	**powerful**

Objective 2. *Explain the use and computation of χ^2 for the one-variable case.*

1.	The single variable application of χ^2 test has been described as a _____ technique.	**goodness-of-fit**
2.	The single variable application of χ^2 determines if there is a significant difference between the _____ and _____ frequencies in each of the table cells.	**observed, expected**
3.	In the single-variable application of χ^2, the expected number of cases falling into each category is determined by the _____.	**null hypothesis**
4.	In the equation for the computation of χ^2 the observed number of cases in a given category is symbolized as_____.	f_o
5.	In the computation of χ^2 the expected number of cases in each category is symbolized as _____.	f_e
6.	When the observed frequencies are identical to the expected frequencies, the value of χ^2 will be_____.	**zero**
7.	When the value of χ^2 is very small, we cannot reject the_____.	**null hypothesis**
8.	As the discrepancy between the observed and expected frequencies increases, we are more likely to _____ the null hypothesis.	**reject**

9.   In the use of χ^2, the degrees of freedom are a function   **cells**
      of the number of _____.

10.   In the use of χ^2, the number of cells is symbolized as _____.   **k**

11.   In the single-variable application of χ^2 the total degrees of freedom   **k - 1**
      is symbolized as _____.

Objective 3. *Explain the limitations in the use of χ^2.*

1.   A basic assumption of χ^2 is that each observation is _____ of all   **independent**
      other observations.

2.   When several observations are made on the same individual   **inflated N**
      and treated as independent observations, the result is an _____.

3.   The requirement of independence within a cell or condition   **statistical**
      is a basic assumption of all _____.   **tests**

4.   The value of χ^2 is directly proportional to the _____.   **sample size**

5.   In the use of χ^2 with one degree of freedom, the expected   **five**
      frequency in all cells should be equal to or greater than _____.

6.   In the use of χ^2 with more than one degree of freedom, the   **80%**
      expected frequency in _____ of the cells should be
      equal to or greater than five.

Objective 4. *Explain the use and computation of three nominal measures of association*
            based on χ^2.

1.   When the variables are statistically independent, the value of χ^2 **zero**
      is _____.

2.   The measure of association for χ^2 that is limited to 2 x 2   **phi**
      contingency tables is the _____.   **coefficient**

3.   The value of the phi coefficient is the square root of the   **N**
      value of χ^2 divided by _____.

4.   The values of the phi coefficient may range from _____ to   **0, 1**
      _____.

5. The phi coefficient is sometimes referred to as a measure of degree of _____. **diagonal concentration**

6. The phi coefficient requires _____ data. **nominal level**

7. The nominal measure of association based on χ^2 that is used primarily for square tables is the _____. **contingency coefficient**

8. The statistician who developed the contingency coefficient was _____. **Pearson**

9. When the variables are independent, the value of the contingency coefficient is equal to _____. **zero**

10. The maximum value of the contingency coefficient is always less than _____. **1**

11. The value of the contingency coefficient is partly determined by the number of _____ and _____ in the contingency table. **rows, columns**

12. The nominal measure of association based on χ^2 for tables of any dimension is _____. **Cramer's V**

13. The values of Cramer's V range from _____ to _____. **0, 1**

14. The denominator of Cramer's V is calculated by multiplication of N and the smaller of the two quantities _____ or _____. **r - 1, c - 1**

15. The most versatile of the three measures of association for χ^2 is _____. **Cramer's V**

Multiple Choice Questions

1. Nonparametric statistics must be substituted for parametric statistics when the variables are measured at the: **b**

    a. ordinal and interval levels
    b. ordinal and nominal levels
    c. ratio and nominal levels
    d. interval and nominal levels

2. The one-variable application of χ^2 is a measure of: **c**

    a. linear regression   c. goodness-of-fit
    b. power efficiency   d. statistical independence

3.   The two-variable application of χ^2 is a measure of: **d**

   a.   linear regression   c.   goodness-of-fit
   b.   power efficiency   d.   statistical independence

4.   In the one-variable application of χ^2, the expected   **d**
   frequencies are dictated by the:

   a.   least squares regression line
   b.   probability of a type II error
   c.   observed frequencies
   d.   null hypothesis

5.   In the two-variable application of χ^2, the expected frequencies   **c**
   are dictated by the:

   a.   least squares regression line
   b.   probability of a type II error
   c.   observed frequencies
   d.   null hypothesis

6.   When the observed frequencies are equal to the expected   **b**
   frequencies, the value of χ^2 will be:

   a.   -1   c. N
   b.   0   d.   1

7.   The maximum possible value of χ^2 is: **c**

   a.   1   c. N
   b.   100   d. k

8.   In the one-variable application of χ^2, the symbol k designates: **a**

   a.   the total number of cells
   b.   the total degrees of freedom
   c.   the total number of observations
   d.   the measure of association for the statistic

9.   In the one-variable application of χ^2, the symbol $k - 1$ designates: **b**

   a.   the total number of cells
   b.   the total degrees of freedom
   c.   the total number of observations
   d.   the measure of association of the statistic

10.   For all degrees of freedom, the shape of the distribution of χ^2 is: **c**

a.   normal   c.   positively skewed
b.   symmetrical   d.   negatively skewed

11.   In the two-variable application of χ^2, the symbols r and c designate: **d**

a.   two measures of association for the statistic
b.   the total degrees of freedom in the contingency table
c.   the total number of observations in the contingency table
d.   the number of rows and columns in the contingency table

12.   In the two-variable application of χ^2, the symbols $(r-1)(c-1)$ **b**
designate:

a.   two measures of association for the statistic
b.   the total degrees of freedom in the contingency table
c.   the total number of observations in the contingency table
d.   the total number of rows and columns in the contingency
       table

13.   The total degrees of freedom in a 6 x 8 contingency table is: **b**

a.   24   c.   48
b.   35   d.   63

14.   In the two-variable application of χ^2 the expected frequency   **b**
of a given cell is the:

a.   sum of the two common marginal frequencies divided
       by N
b.   product of the two common marginal frequencies divided
       by N
c.   sum of the two common marginal frequencies multiplied
       by N
d.   product of the two common marginal frequencies multiplied
       by N

15.   In the two-variable application of χ^2 the total of the expected   **b**
frequencies is:

a.   larger than the number of observed frequencies
b.   equal to the total number of observed frequencies
c.   less than the number of observed frequencies
d. $2N$

16. In the two-variable application of χ^2 the expected frequencies for each column and row are: **b**

   a. larger than the observed frequencies for the same columns and rows
   b. equal to the observed frequencies for the same columns and rows
   c. less than the observed frequencies for the same columns and rows
   d. equal to N

17. When several observations on the same individual are treated as independent observations, the result is: **c**

   a. an increased probability of a type II error
   b. a reduction in power
   c. an inflated N
   d. a decreased probability of a type II error

18. The value of χ^2 is directly proportional to the :   **b**

   a. significance level
   b. sample size
   c. probability of a type II error
   d. number of cells in the contingency table

19. In the use of χ^2 with one degree of freedom, the expected frequencies in all cells must be equal to or greater than: **b**

   a. 1   c. 10
   b. 5   d. 20

20. When using χ^2 with more than one degree of freedom, the expected frequency in all cells must be equal to or greater than five for at least _____ of the cells?   **c**

   a. 60%   c. 80%
   b. 70%   d. 90%

21. An appropriate measure of association for χ^2 with 2 x 2 contingency tables is the: **b**

   a. contingency coefficient   c. Robert's Z
   b. phi coefficient   d. theta coefficient

22. An appropriate measure of association for X^2 with square   **a**
    contingency tables having more than two rows and columns
    is the:

    a.   contingency coefficient   c.   Robert's Z
    b.   phi coefficient   d.   theta coefficient

23. The appropriate measure of association for a larger contingency   **c**
    table of any size is the:

    a.   contingency coefficient   c.   Cramer's V
    b.   phi coefficient   d.   theta coefficient

24. Which of the following measures of association has a PRE   **b**
    interpretation?

    a.   the contingency coefficient
    b.   the phi coefficient
    c.   Cramer's V
    d.   the theta coefficient

25. The value of the phi coefficient is the square root of X^2 **d**

    a.   added to N c.   multiplied by N
    b.   subtracted from N d.   divided by N

26. Which of the following measures of association has a   **b**
    maximum value that is always less than 1?

    a.   the phi coefficient
    b.   the contingency coefficient
    c.   Goodman and Kruskal's gamma
    d.   Cramer's V

27. Which of the following is the most versatile measure of association   **b**
    for X^2?

    a.   Goodman and Kruskal's gamma
    b.   Cramer's V
    c.   the phi coefficient
    d.   the contingency coefficient

28. In a 2 x 2 chi-square table, the observed frequency for each cell   **d**
is 20. Total frequency is 80. The expected frequency for the
cell in column 1, row 1 is:

    a.   40   c.   10
    b.   80   d.   20

29. The general rule of thumb for ascertaining the degrees of   **c**
freedom for all contingency-type tables with two variables
when computing (chi square) is:

    a. $df = (r - 2)(c - 1)$
    b. $df = (r - 2)(c - 2)$
    c. $df = (r - 1)(c - 1)$
    d. $df = (r)(c - 2)$

30. In a 2 x 2 chi-square test, how many degrees of freedom are there: **b**

    a.   0   c.   2
    b.   1   d.   3

31. In the X^2 one-variable case, if $N = 1001$ and $k = 4$, the number   **d**
of degrees of freedom is:

    a.   1000   c.   4
    b.   3000   d.   3

32. In the X^2 test of independence, $N = 101$, $r = 3$, $c = 2$, the number of   **c**
degrees of freedom is:

    a.   100   c.   2
    b.   202   d.   3

33. Which of the following is a nonparametric test?   **b**

    a. t c. z
    b.   chi-square   d.   none of the above

Computational Problem

1. An investigator was interested in determining if the ratio of men to women at a
particular company was independent of race. Of 100 randomly selected whites, 58
were male, and of 100 African-Americans, 40 were male. Using $\alpha = .01$, what did she
conclude?

Answer
Computational Problem

1.

	Male	Female	Row sum
White	58 (49)	42 (51)	100
African-American	40 (49)	60 (51)	100
Column sum	98	102	200

$\chi^2 = (58 - 49)^2/49 + (42 - 51)^2/51 + (40 - 49)^2/49 + (60 - 51)^2/51 =$ 1.653 + 1.588 + 1.653 + 1.588 = 6.482. Because the obtained χ^2 does not exceed 6.635 at $df = 1$, we cannot reject H_o. Differential hiring of male and female African-Americans and whites is not practiced.

Chapter 17

STATISTICAL INFERENCE: ORDINALLY SCALED VARIABLES

Learning Objectives

After mastering the content of this chapter, you should be able to:

1. *Explain the concept of statistical inference with ordinally scaled variables and name the techniques that are frequently employed as alternatives to parametric tests.*

2. *Explain the uses and computation of the Mann-Whitney U-Test.*

3. *Explain the uses of nonparametric tests involving correlated samples.*

4. *Explain the uses and computation of the Sign-Test.*

5. *Explain the uses and computation of the Wilcoxon Matched Pairs Signed-Rank Test.*

Programmed Review

Objective 1. *Explain the concept of statistical inference with ordinally scaled variables and name the techniques that are frequently employed as alternative to parametric tests.*

1. The Mann-Whitney U-Test, the Sign-Test, and the Wilcoxon Matched-Pairs Signed-Rank Test are often used as_____ to parametric tests.

    alternatives

2. The Mann-Whitney U-Test is used in situations where two groups are_____.

    independent

3. The Sign-Test is used in situations where groups are _____.

    correlated

4. The Sign-Test utilizes information concerning the _____ of the difference between pairs of scores.

    direction

5. The Wilcoxon Matched-Pairs Signed-Rank Test uses matched _____ with scores that are _____.

    pairs, quantitative

Objective 2. *Explain the uses and computation of the Mann-Whitney U-Test.*

1. When measurements fail to achieve interval scaling or when the researcher wishes to avoid parametric assumptions, the Mann-Whitney U-Test is used as an alternative to the _____.

    Student's *t*-ratio

2. If there is no difference between groups, the order of groups should be _____.

    random

3. The Mann-Whitney test is concerned with the _____ of the statistic U.

    sampling distribution

4. To find U you must first _____ all of scores from the lowest to highest.

    rank

5. The procedures for converting tied scores to ranks are the same as is used for the _____ statistic.

    Spearman's r_s

6. If the sample sizes of both groups are approximately equal, and exceed 20, the _____ may be used to evaluate the significance of the difference between ranks.

    z-statistic

Objective 3. *Explain the uses of nonparametric tests involving correlated samples.*

1. A correlated-samples design is also referred to as a _____ design.

    matched-group

2. A correlated-samples design is one in which pairs of respondents are matched on a variable that is known to be correlated with the _____ .

    dependent variable

3. A correlated-samples design ensures that he groups are _____.

    equivalent

4. A correlated-samples design permits the _____ of the effects of the correlated variable.

    removal

5. A correlated-samples design allows for the reduction in the level of measurement _____ .

    error

Objective 4. *Explain the uses and computation of the Sign-Test.*

1. The Sign-Test is a nonparametric statistical test for_____ scaled variables.

    ordinally

2. The Sign-Test is used with matched or _____ samples.

    correlated

3. The Sign-Test is a variation of the _____ test presented earlier in the text.

    binomial

4. The Sign-Test assumes that pairs of measurements must be _____ of each other.

    independent

5. A disadvantage of the Sign-Test is that it eliminates _____ information from the data.

    quantitative

6. With the Sign-Test all _____ are treated as if they are the same regardless of the sign of the difference.

    differences

Objective 5. *Explain the uses and computation of the Wilcoxon Matched Pairs Signed-Rank Test.*

1. The Wilcoxon matched-pairs signed-rank test achieves greater power by utilizing _____ information.

    quantitative

2. The Wilcoxon matched-pairs signed-rank test assumes that the scale of measurement is _____.

    ordinal

3.	The Wilcoxon matched-pairs signed-rank test also assumes	**ordinal**
	that the difference in scores constitutes an _____ scale.

4.	When all the assumptions are met, the Wilcoxon matched-pairs	**sensitive**
	signed-rank test is a extremely _____ test for obtaining
	probability values.

Multiple Choice Questions

1.	Assume: two conditions, experimental and control; respondents	**d**
	assigned at random to experimental conditions; scale of
	measurement ordinal or higher; assumption of normality cannot
	be maintained. The appropriate test statistic is:

	a.	student's *r*-ratio for uncorrelated samples
	b.	Wilcoxon's matched-pairs signed-rank test
	c.	the sign test
	d.	Mann-Whitney *U*

2.	Assume: two conditions, experimental and control; matched	**c**
	respondents; scale of measurement ordinal, in which paired
	scores indicate only the direction of a difference; assumption
	of normality cannot be maintained. The appropriate test statistic is:

	a.	student's *t*-ratio for uncorrelated samples
	b.	Wilcoxon's matched pairs signed-rank test
	c.	the sign test
	d.	Mann-Whitney *U*

3.	Assume: two conditions, experimental and control; matched	**b**
	respondents; scale is ordinal, in which the difference in scores is
	also ordinal; assumption of normality cannot be maintained.
	The appropriate test statistic is:

	a.	student's *t*-ratio for uncorrelated samples
	b.	Wilcoxon matched-pairs signed-rank test
	c.	the sign test
	d.	none of the above

4.	In the Wilcoxon test we should drop any pairs with a	**b**

	a.	negative difference
	b.	zero difference
	c.	negligible difference
	d.	positive Mann-Whitney *U*

5.   Given: the scores of two independent groups of respondents in   **b**
     a study; scale of measurement is ratio; scores are skewed to the
     right. The appropriate test statistic is:

     a.   student's t-ratio
     b.   Mann-Whitney U
     c.   the sign test
     d.   Wilcoxon's matched-pairs signed-rank test

6.   Given the following scores for two groups: Group E, 8, 12, 15, 17;   **d**
     Group C, 2, 4, 7, 9, 10; and
     $$U = N_1 N_2 + \frac{N_1(N_1 + 1)}{2} - R_1,$$
     U equals:
     a.   7   c.   -22
     b.   2   d.   none of the above

7.   Given: $N_1 = 5$, $N_2 = 5$, $\alpha = 0.05$, two-tailed test, and the critical   **a**
     value of $U \leq 2$ or ≥ 23, we obtain a U of 24. We should:

     a.   reject H_o
     b.   fail to reject H_o
     c.   depends on whether we have obtained U or U'
     d.   recalculate

8.   Given the following ratings assigned to respondents before and after
     the introduction of the experimental variable:

Before	15	13	10	9	7	6	5	4	2
After	12	11	6	7	8	3	1	6	0

     Employing the sign-test, $\alpha = 0.05$, two tailed test, we conclude: **b**
     a.   we must reject the H_o
     b.   we must accept the H_o
     c.   the experimental conditions had a small effect
     d.   the experimental conditions resulted in lowered ratings

9.   Applying the Wilcoxon matched-pairs signed-rank test to the   **c**
     data in problem 8, we obtain a T of:

     a.   3   c.   4.5
     b.   31.5   d.   36

10.   A disadvantage of the sign test when applied to ordinally scaled   **d**
       variables is that:

       a.   It is frequently difficult to determine the direction of a change.
       b.   Pairs of measurements must be independent of one another
       c.   It increases the risk of a Type I error.
       d.   It does not utilize any quantitative information inherent in the
             data.

11.   A disadvantage or applying the Wilcoxon matched-pairs signed-   **d**
       ranked test to ordinally scaled data is that:

       a.   It does not utilize information concerning the direction of
             the differences.
       b.   It losses sight of magnitude of differences.
       c.   Pairs of measurements must be independent of one another.
       d.   None of the above

12.   The test of significance which employs the binomial sampling   **a**
       distribution to arrive at probability values is:

       a.   the sign test
       b.   the Wilcoxon matched-pairs signed-rank test
       c.   the Mann-Whitney U
       d.   none of the above

13.   An alternative to the Student's t-ratio for uncorrelated samples when   **c**
       measurements fail to achieve interval scaling or when one wishes to
       avoid the assumptions of parametric counterpart is:

       a.   Wilcoxon's matched-pairs signed-rank test
       b.   Robert's Rule
       c.   the Mann-Whitney U
       d.   the sign test

14.   Given the following:

Rank	1	2	3	4	5	6	7	8	9	10
Condition	C	C	C	E	C	C	E	C	E	E

       The Mann-Whitney U and U', respectively, are: **a**
       a.   4, 20   c.   4, 15
       b.   9, 15   d.   9, 20

15.   Which statistical test does not belong with the group?   c

    a.   the sign test
    b.   Wilcoxon's matched-pair signed-rank test
    c.   Robert's Rule
    d.   Mann-Whitney U